A Preacher's Daughter Looking for Love

Written by: J. Delores Williams

Anderson Inc. Publishing
P O Box 37881
Jacksonville, Fl. 32236

A Preacher's Daughter Looking for Love

Written by: J. Delores Williams

Published By:
Anderson Inc. Publishing
P.O. Box 37881
Jacksonville, FL 32236

ALL RIGHTS RESERVED

No part of this book may be reproduced or transmitted in any form or by any means- electronic or mechanical, including photocopying, recording, or by any information storage and retrieved system without written permission from the authors, except for the inclusion of brief quotations in a review.

The publication is designed to provide accurate and authoritative information about the subject matter covered. It is sold with the understanding the publisher is not engaged in rendering legal, accounting, or other professional services. If legal advice or other expert assistance is required, the services of a competent professional person should be sought.

Anderson Inc. Publishing Books are available at special discounts for bulk purchases, sales promotions, fundraisers, or educational purposes.

Email: andersoninc@netzero.com

About the Author:

J. Delores Williams is a native of Alabama. She is the mother of two adult children and three grandchildren.

J. Delores has a passion for God and people. She enjoys reading and has found a new passion for writing. There are no challenges too hard for her to tackle.

J. Delores believes that everyone should be happy. Her philosophy is that God gave everyone one life to live and we should all live it to the fullest. Also, everyone has something to contribute whether it's a smile or just saying thank you. J. Delores believes that the good that we do will always come back to us.

J. Delores is a true living testimony that proves prayer really works.

Acknowledgments

I would like to thank my dear friend
Mr. Anthony M. Anderson Sr.
for seeing something in me and
for believing in me.

When I met Mr. Anderson I was living in the
hood next door to the drug dealers, and
across the street from another drug dealer,
he did not judge me by my surrounding,
but he judged me by my character,
For him to trust me enough to do this for
me knowing I didn't have any money.

I will forever be grateful for his friendship,
patience, time, and love. In addition, thanks
to his little girl who is always with him. Again,
I say thanks and may God richly bless and
keep you. May his face continue to shine
upon you.

Dedication and Thanks

*I would like to thank my friend Debra Lewis for being there for me.
She invited me to my first book club.
She pulled me and pushed me but I just was not ready to go.*

Thanks Debra

I dedicate my first book to Florina and Frank Steward; they have always believed in me and have done everything in their power to help me make it. God Bless!

Table of Contents

Dedication 5

Chapter 1 - It is all about Tiff 7

Chapter 2 - The Dating Game 9

Chapter 3 – Marriage 30

Chapter 4 - Gavin, God Sent 66

Chapter 5 - New House, New Start 82

Chapter 6 - California Get-A-Way 93

    Being Submissive 101
    The Party 105
    Sunday Morning 107
    The Family 110

Chapter 7 - Back to Tiff's World 118

Chapter 8 – Tiff's fantasy 129

Chapter 1
It's all about Tiff

I would like to tell you about my God sent man, how wonderful he is, and how precious he is. However, let me first share some of my past relationships with you so you can see why I know he is God sent.

Tiffany was the second of six children; her father was a holiness preacher. They believed in the power of prayer. Tiffany felt that her parents had the best marriage and the best relationship.

Tiffany is brown but she always thought she was high yellow, she thought she was the finest person out there, big legs, small waist, big pretty brown eyes and a smile that would make any man light up.

When Tiffany walked out of her house, everything had to match including her hair. Tiffany had to have a new car every two years. She always worked hard, made good money to indulge Tiffany. She had long wigs, short wigs, blond wigs, black wigs, red wigs and brown wigs. She just knew she was all of that. Tiffany was told she looked like her mother and to Tiffany her mother was very pretty, to children all mothers are pretty.

When she walked into a room, she lit the room up with her tight fitting jeans and loud voice. Tiffany thought this was her world.

Tiffany was a darn good sales person; she sold make-up and jewelry, life, health, and auto insurance. Tiffany worked the southern region: Mississippi, Louisiana, Arkansas, and Texas. Every state she worked in she had to have a man: Doctors, Businessmen, Salesmen, and Janitors. The only requirement was they had to have a job and willing to spend money on her. Tiff (Tiffany's nickname) always wanted to be married to a man who loved and adored her. The men who choose her or who she choose, were stupid, ugly, mouth problems or just wimps. Tiff never listened to anyone, but she would appreciate a man who was talking about something.

Chapter 2
The Dating Game

Tiff was working in Ponchatoula, Louisiana when she met Benny. Benny drove a beautiful white Cadillac; he asked her if he could come to Slidell one Sunday and take her to dinner. Tiff said why not. Benny told Tiff that she was pretty, Tiff said I know. Benny came to Slidell and they went out for dinner. His car was shining, once he put his hands on the steering wheel Tiff knew then she just could not do him. Benny had so much dirt under his fingernails (it looked like oil or something). You would think if a brother took a sister out on a first date he would fix up a little bit.

Tiff and Benny went to the restaurant and as they were eating, she kept looking at Benny's hands, Tiff was quiet, he asked her what was wrong, she told him the food was making her sick. She asked him if he would take her home. He told her he was thinking about getting a room, Tiff feels sick because she could not see Benny putting his hands on her me clothes, and God knows not her body. After he pulls up in front of her house, she jumps out and run inside. Benny knocks on the door and tells Tiff's father that the food made her sick.

Benny says to her father, I hope she feels better; ask her to call me later. After Benny leaves, Tiff's father calls her and asks her what she has done now. Tiff said, daddy did you see his hands. Tiff's father said, those hands are workers hands. Tiff said to her father, if Benny had touched her, he would have gotten her clothes and body dirty.

A couple of months later, a young man named Michael, one of Tiff's co-workers, asked her to go to the Christmas party with him. Tiff said yes. Tiff had no intention of going with him. Tiff being Tiff is just being a flirt. The night of the party Tiff washed her hair. The young man knocked on the door and when Tiff's mother opened the door, there stood Michael all dressed up with a corsage in his hand. He asked for Tiff, Tiff's mother thought, what has she done this time. Tiff comes to the door as if she has done nothing wrong. Tiff thought Michael knew she was playing with him because he knew she was a preacher's kid and she did not do parties. After Michael left, Tiff's mother looked at her and shook her head, told her she was an embarrassment to the family. Tiff told her mother if she had gone to the party and everybody knew that she was the preacher's kid that would have been the embarrassment.

Tiff's father told her mother that Tiff did have a point. Tiff promised her parents she would do better. Three months passed and Tiff was good. Jonathan, Tiff's brother, told her that his best friend Robert wanted to take her out. Tiff asked Jonathan what kind of man was his friend; he told Tiff he was a nice person. Robert, Jonathan's friend, promised him if he hooked him up with Tiff he would be a gentleman. He thought she was sexy. Robert called Tiff and they made the date, when he came to pick her up, he looked very nice but he had bad breath, also he brought Tiff flowers and they went to a nice restaurant. After dinner, Tiff tried to give him a mint or gum but he said candy and mints mess your teeth up. Tiff almost said your mouth already smells. The night was short because Tiff told him she had to go to work early the next day. Tiff gets home, blasted Jonathan, and asked him why he set her up like that. He told Tiff everything she asked him about Robert he gave true answers. He told Tiff she did not ask about his breath.

JJ is Tiff's brother-in-law; he is married to her sister, Virginia. He works at the Mill; Harold, a nice preacher man, asked him if he knew a lady that was cute, sweet and saved like his wife, because he was looking for a wife.

He told Harold about his sister-in-law Tiff. Tiff gave JJ permission to give Harold her phone number. Harold and Tiff spoke a few times; he told JJ that she sounds like his kind of woman. JJ asked Virginia to prepare dinner one Sunday and invite Tiff and Harold. Virginia bought Tiff a dress to put on, just in case Tiff's dress "was not saved enough". Harold showed up at Tiff's door with a dozen fresh eggs, Tiff smiled. Harold told her the eggs were from his chickens. Tiff invited him in and offered him coffee, as they drank the coffee, he told her that he had inherited a farm from his father. Tiff said to herself, oh hell no, she could not and never will slop a pig. Tiff says it is time to leave because he did not impress her. Harold opened the car door for Tiff and then he gets in the car. Harold drives a grey Coup-Deville; it was so clean. Harold is tall, good looking, pretty teeth, shoes shined, and hands clean. Harold starts the car, as Tiff listens to the music, she asked Harold if that's the radio or his tape. He said a tape; she wanted to know if that was a service he had attended, He said, no. Tiff asked him, what is it? He said the Lord told him to buy and learn the tongues tape fluently. Tiff told him he was lying and tongues were a gift from God. Tiff jumped in her preaching mode.

Tiff start preaching about what happened on the day of Pentecost. When they arrived at JJ and Virginia's home, the food was good. Virginia served fried chicken, potato salad, corn, green beans, and macaroni and cheese. Tiff found out later that most of that stuff came from Harold's farm. After spending three hours there, Harold told JJ and Virginia that the food was very good and thanked JJ again for introducing Tiff to him. Tiff said nothing because she was thinking about hogs, chickens, and cows. Tiff knew if he had fresh food, she had to get her nails dirty when digging in the ground.

As Harold and Tiff rode back to her house, Harold asked her, if she thought she would ever marry. Tiff told him she just had not found the right man. Harold looked at Tiff and said, the bible says, "whoso findeth a wife, findeth a good thing and obtaineth favour of the Lord", not she who findeth a husband. Tiff knew Harold was a preacher, he told JJ and JJ told Tiff's parents. Harold looked at Tiff and asked her, (if she married) what kind of man would she be looking for, and what did she expect from him? Tiff told Harold she was looking for a man who did not drink, smoke, nor use drugs. Harold told Tiff she was looking at the man. Tiff also told Harold, God first, Tiff second, the church and everybody and everything after her. Harold said wait a minute Sister Tiff, God and the church goes together. Tiff said nope, you got it twisted. Tiff pulls out another sermon, "so goes the home, so goes the church, God is head of the house, man is head of his family," that didn't even go there but this is Tiff's conversation.

Harold looks at Tiff and asks her "do you think you're supposed to come before God's people?" he did not realize he had struck a nerve, Tiff asked him how do you see me, you do not see me as one of God's children. He was trying to explain it but he could not. Tiff also asked Harold, do you mean you will be at church shouting the victory and your family will be home needing bread. He said no Sister Tiff, everything that you will need to bake bread, you will have. Tiff was thinking about baking bread, slopping hogs, feeding chickens, ringing chicken heads off and milking cows. Tiff had nothing else to say on the conversation. After Harold brought Tiff home, he walked her to the door, kissed her on the cheek, and said, good night my princess. Tiff called her mother and tells her about the evening, of course, Virginia had given a completely different story. Tiff told her mother the man had hogs, chickens, cows, horses, and a garden.

Tiff told her mother she could not do him. Tiff's mother asked her what was she looking for. Tiff just said, he is not the one.

A couple of weeks passed and Tiff's father was invited to preach at a church in Laurel, Mississippi, he asked Harold if he would go with him and bring the word. Harold lived sixty miles from Slidell, Louisiana, Tiff was so happy that her father invited him because then they will see what Tiff was trying to say. After Sunday school, at Tiff's father church, the saints were coming outside when Harold pulls up in his pretty car. Tiff's father asked everybody to start loading up their cars. At that time, Tiff was driving a red and white Mustang. They knew the young man in the coup was for Tiff, he was tall and nice looking. The young women got in his car; they did not have a clue what they were running into. Tiff mother and three ladies rode with Tiff.

Harold walks to Tiff's car and asked her how she was feeling, Tiff said, fine. Harold asked her if she had problems with the young women riding with him. Tiff said, no. He kissed her on the jaw and then walked to his car. Tiff smiles and tells her mother to watch the difference in the ladies on the ride back home.

They got to the church in Laurel; the singing was excellent. Tiff's father stands and says, "he has a treat for the congregation", he has brought a young fireball preacher from Louisiana, let us all receive him by standing on your feet. Tiff's family did not know everything about Harold. Harold was white except his color. He got saved in a white country church a few years ago and plays tapes every day trying to play catch up. Harold got up trying to preach, he was black, but he had so much white down in him. He was trying so hard to sound black, reciting his learned tongues. His high points were still very low. He had an alter call and he had to speak in tongues in everybody's life. Tiff just sat there and looked at him.

After church, they asked all the preachers and their spouses to go to the preachers study to eat. Harold found Tiff and asked her how did he do. Tiff looked at him and smiled, he did not know what to read in her smile. Tiff wanted to say that's not your calling, but she didn't care to hurt his feelings. Harold told the preachers that Tiff was his future wife. Tiff did not expect that. She knew she was not going to slop no hogs, feed no chickens, nor milk any cows. Tiff had nothing to say because it was not happening.

Harold told the preachers whom he did not know until that day, that Tiff needed a little more training in that area. Tiff said nothing; she just looked at her mother.

After the fellowship, Alberta, one of the young women who jumped in the car with Harold, came to Tiff and apologized for being disrespectful. Alberta asked Tiff, if she would please let her drive her car home. The young people wanted to ride in Tiff's car. They did not want to listen to Harold's tapes again. Tiff left her mother in her car because they wasn't going to hear the music they wanted to play in Tiff's car. They didn't know Harold played tongues tapes when he had to preach. Tiff knew he was playing them louder, the fact that he had to preach in a black church. Tiff and the three ladies rode with Harold.

The ride home was the same, he was talking about how the anointing fell upon the people, and he looked at Tiff and said, Sister Tiff you have to get with it. Sister Beck said, you just leave her alone. She got more religion than you. Tiff asked her to leave it alone because he was just playing. Harold said, no I wasn't. That is not a saved outfit you are wearing today. Tiff asked as humble as she knew how, what is wrong with what I have on.

Harold said, for one thing you have on silk stockings, and fake nails, there is nothing fake in the kingdom. He said, she needs to take a lesson from the white minister's wife because the blacks just don't have it.

Tiff still talking low and sweet, she asked Harold why we have black and white churches, since the white folks got all the answers. Sister Minnie sat up on her seat and shook her finger in Harold's face, she told him don't you ever as long as you live talk to this child like that. Sister Money said, he doesn't know anything about Tiff. He and nobody else are going to put her in no cotton stockings, unless that is what she wants. Sister Beck said, nobody but nobody talk to Tiff that way. Tiff was saying to herself, go girls. That reminded Tiff of the old school days; she never had to fight.

The rest of the ride home was quiet. Tiff asked Harold how many black churches had he spoken in, he didn't answer her. Sister Beck said, I know you hear her talking to you. Tiff was only being messy; he said nothing else to Tiff. After they got to the church everybody got out, he asked Tiff to get out so he could leave. Tiff told him, she wasn't getting out until he talked to her. Harold said in a stern voice, "get out Tiff".

Tiff said no because she hadn't done anything. He told Tiff to get out, Tiff said just take me home. Tiff rolled her window down and asked Alberta to bring her car to her tomorrow morning. Tiff asked Harold to take her home please. Harold started his car again and drove in complete silence. When he pulled up in front of Tiff's house, Tiff opened the door to get out. Harold took her by the hand and asked her to sit for a while. Tiff could not understand why he was so angry, there were a whole lot of times that Tiff could have lost it, but instead, she just held her peace. Harold asked Tiff to look at him. Harold told Tiff he need her in his life and he told Tiff she was good for him. He asked Tiff to marry him. Tiff looked Harold in his face, eyeball to eyeball, she told Harold, she don't do chickens, she is not going to slop no hogs, she will not gather eggs nor will she milk the cows.

Tiff told Harold, you have said nothing about love. Tiff said I might be good for you but you are not good for me. Harold told Tiff that he would teach her how to be a good domestic wife since her mother did not teach her, he said, no offence Tiff. Tiff said nothing. Harold told Tiff once he shows her one time, she will get the hang of things, and she will not have to work away from home.

Tiff could have taken a seven day a week job ten hours a day and still would not be as tired as she would be in one day on the farm.

Tiff told Harold he was a good catch for a woman who had many kids and nowhere to go. Then and only then, a woman would be grateful for the offer. Tiff told him she could see them going to divorce court, and she just did not want to put him through that. Harold told Tiff he would not leave her, and as long as she lives, she will always be a part of the farm.

Tiff said, Harold, you may not leave me, but I know I will leave you. I know what the bible says about divorce, only for fornication, Tiff said not only would I be too tired to fornicate, I will be too tired to satisfy you. Tiff said, Harold, I just can't; I need more than you are willing to give me. Harold asked her, how many black men have as much as he has to offer a woman. Tiff said, that is why the divorce rate is so high among black families because the black man cannot give himself, his love, or his devotion to his woman. Tiff said you never mentioned giving me any of that.

Tiff told him, if she married him, without him giving her what she needed, he would be working and she would still be looking for love. He asked Tiff if she had a strong sex drive, Tiff said it's not about sex, it's about being together. Harold, with you coming home every week from working in New Orleans, you could quit your job and we can both work the land. Harold said, God has not given him that assignment just yet. Tiff said, God has not given it to me either. She did not want to do it. Harold said, will you just pray about it and see what God is saying, Tiff said, God is speaking, he is saying for me not to wreck your future and your life.

Tiff knows she is hard headed and stubborn, she does not have to live in a land of dictatorship. Tiff tells Harold that he is a dictator. Tiff gets out of Harold's car knowing without a doubt that she had done the right thing. Let him be disappointed now instead of later on. Tiff called her mother and said, she will no longer be seeing Harold. Tiff's mother said he is very crazy, she repeated what the young folk told her that happened, as did her friends who rode with them.
Tiff's mother said she is going to stop riding Tiff so hard.

Tiff's mother asked her what she was looking for, she said, I will tell you when I find it. I will know it and it will not take me a long time to know it.

After that relationship, Tiff just went on being Tiff. It has never taken her longer than three weeks at the most to get over a relationship. Tiff thought if she was in a relationship with Gavin, and things did not go right, Gavin would have to call for a plea bargain, she knew she could not walk away.

Tiff relocated to Arkansas to work at Anderson Insurance Company and to have fun being Tiff. Mr. Gibbs, the staff manager, wants to introduce her to his friend, Marlon; he and his wife arranged for Marlon and Tiff to meet at the country club. Tiff was feeling like a high roller. Marlon came in with his long gown on; it was real pretty and rare. When they told Tiff he was Marlon, Tiff stood up. Once Marlon got to the table and saw Tiff, he got on his knees and kissed her hand and said, welcome My Lady! Tiff blushed; Marlon was very professional. He sat down and placed his napkin in his lap before they ate.

He asked Tiff to let him order for her because there was a special dish he would love for her to try. Marlon was ugly, but he was so cool. Tiff said to herself, if he took the dress off and put on pants, she could do him.

Soft jazz was playing, Marlon asked Tiff to dance. Marlon held Tiff as if she was a piece of china; Tiff was eating it all up. Marlon was about thirty years older than she was, but he was a cool old man. He told her for the last twenty years he has been living in Africa. However, he decided to move back to the states. Marlon said he would love to see her again; he was cool and his conversation was interesting. After being in Arkansas, Tiff and the insurance gang had to go to a meeting in Shreveport, La.; some of the cars were not up to par. Tiff told the gang she would use her car. Tiff told Marlon about the trip, Marlon told her he would love to take the trip with her. Tiff thought well, because she would not have to pay for her room. Tiff picked Marlon up first; she told him two of the ladies from the office were riding with her.

Marlon said to Tiff, why didn't you tell me. Tiff told him she was telling him now, he got so upset, and Tiff reminds him this is her job and not a pleasure trip.

Tiff asked Marlon what was he going to do, he asked Tiff what did she want. Tiff told him it did not matter, the job is her bread and butter, you cannot work with people and expect to get good response and not help if you can. Tiff asked Marlon what was the big deal. Marlon asked Tiff if she saw the office manager going out of the way making sure everybody had a ride. Tiff told him they talked the night before, and she assured the office manager that they would get there on time. Marlon asked Tiff to take him back home. Tiff made a u-turn, took him home and that was that. Tiff thought he is old, short-patience and selfish.

The trip to Shreveport, LA. was fun and business. Tiff met people from other districts; they told her it would be a pleasure to work with her. Tiff gave her best when it came to her job, because that was her bread and butter. Tiff returned home to Slidell, LA., while there she visited the hospital with a friend; as they passed this one room, Tiff looked in and saw a person all jacked up, sounded like they was crying. Tiff walked in the room and noticed it was a man, being Tiff, she asked the man what's wrong, Tiff said he was acting like his best friend had just died, the man waited, and said, I have lost my best friend and he said no more.

Tiff asked, was it your dog or your mother? he waited; he said my mother. Tiff said Oh my God! I am sorry. Would you tell me what happened, he said why I should tell you, Tiff said because I want to know. The man said if I told you, how would it help my pain? Tiff said it may release some anger, or maybe a little of your pain. The man said my name is Lindsey, my mother, sister, and my only brother was killed in a car accident returning from our aunt's funeral; I was driving. Tiff said to herself why did I ask. He said he was not able to make any of the funerals. Lindsey told Tiff he broke his collarbone, both legs and both arms. He told Tiff when the car caught on fire he was burned so bad, until they had to graft skin off his butt to save his face. Tiff told Lindsey when people kiss him he do not have to tell them to kiss his butt, they automatically do. He told Tiff you got it. Tiff said Jesus! Tiff could not stand to hear anymore, she told Lindsey she had to leave; he asked her if she was a nurse, she said no. He asked her name. She told him Tiff, He said that was a pretty name. Tiff said thanks. Lindsey asked if she would visit with him again. Tiff said sure why not. He told Tiff no one tried to understand him in the hospital, he said he had been there three months.
Tiff left Lindsey's room and had to lean on the wall for a little while.

The nurses looked at her, they wanted to know if Tiff knew him, Tiff told them no. The nurse said we see he can talk. Tiff said yes, the nurse asked Tiff what was his name, Tiff told the nurse, his name is Lindsey. Tiff goes home tell her mother about the man she met at the hospital. Tiffs mother asked Tiff if she was going to heal him, save him, and marry him. Tiff told her mother, that was not a bad idea. Tiff laid in bed that night and asked God why so much pain. She asked God should she get involved.

A week later Tiff went back to the hospital to see Lindsey, he was about the same she asked him how he felt, and he told her like crap. Tiff told him that was not a good answer, he told her that's how it is. Tiff told Lindsey the people here at the hospital do not think you can talk. Lindsey told Tiff there is nothing to talk about. Tiff asked Lindsey May I ask you a question, Lindsey said to Tiff ask him anything. Tiff asked Lindsey if he was a believer, Lindsey asked Tiff a believer in what. Tiff said in Jesus, Lindsey asked Tiff who is he? Tiff said God's son, Lindsey asked Tiff who is he, Tiff said he is our creator, Lindsey said I never heard of him.
Tiff wondered to herself. Is he serious or is he bitter or do he not know any better.

Tiff asked Lindsey did he attend church before the accident, he asked Tiff what is that. Tiff said to Lindsey I have one more question and I will leave you alone. Lindsey said go on and I have a few questions to ask you. Tiff told Lindsey, there is a little book that's called the Bible, and the Bible talks about God, Jesus, and the Holy Spirit. Tiff asked in her most serious fine voice would you please let me come a few minutes each day to share the love of God with you. Lindsey asked Tiff starting when? Tiff asked Lindsey for him to set the time. Lindsey said no it is on you because I have nothing but time. Tiff asked Lindsey should she call before she came, he told her no because he does not answer no phone.

Tiff left asking herself what she has gotten herself into. As Tiff walked to her car, checking her appointment book, the only time she had was the three o clock appointment she had to get her nails done; now she had to make a decision, what was more important her nails or his soul, Tiff said to herself I have to sleep on this one. As Tiff fell asleep, she dreamed that someone was calling her name.

Tiff woke up; she said that must have been the sign for her to go study the word with Lindsey.

Tiff thought if that was Gavin, she would have paid for an extra bed to be put in his room and she would have read to him and stroked him all night.

Tiff got to the hospital at three fifteen, she entered Lindsey's room with her small testament, and she asked Lindsey how was he feeling? He said like crap. Tiff asked Lindsey did he believe she was coming back, he told her he never gave her nor the Bible Studies any thought. Tiff said to Lindsey, she would love to start it off with a prayer did he mind, he did not answer. Tiff made it short she said, "Lord we thank you for this day and this opportunity. Amen."

Lindsey asked Tiff, if there is a God, why so much pain, why did he take my family and just leave me? Lindsey asked Tiff why did her God take his wife two weeks ago who had been battling breast cancer? He said answer me that before you go any farther. Tiff said ok. Let's first talk about the wife; your wife had cancer before the accident, right, God knew you were not able to care of her, and she was not able to take care of you. The next question, Lindsey asked Tiff if she was going to screw up the other questions the way she just did the last one, please just leave.

Tiff told Lindsey she thought that was a good answer. Lindsey told Tiff that was a bad answer and asked her not to come back to visit with him anymore. Tiff told Lindsey she will be back, but not this week.

Chapter 3
Marriage

Tiff met Alex in a small town in Louisiana and he was 18 years older. He gave Tiff everything she thought she wanted, watches, rings, cell phones, he always took her shopping, kept her car up and gave her three hundred dollars weekly allowance.

Brenda worked with Tiff, one day Tiff took Brenda to Alex house. He gave Tiff three hundred dollars; Brenda asked Tiff how did she get that kind of money from Alex without asking? Tiff told Brenda you have to be cute, that is all. After Tiff spends one night in Alex arms, he asked her to marry him promising her the world. Alex was a successful businessman, in other words, he was a big fish in a small pond. He was 5 feet 9 inches tall, nice looking and pleasant to be around. Tiff and Alex got married; they had a large church wedding, and good food. Tiff told Alex she didn't know how to cook and he told her that's ok as long as she knew how to make love. The city population was 15,000; 17 whites to every one black. After Tiffany married Alex, she learned that he had two ex-wives and seven kids all in that small city. Everybody knew Tiff as wife number three.

Three women in the same small city answering to the same name, Wow! Alex loved Tiff, but there was always so much drama. The kids were small; the kids had to spend nights with Alex and Tiff. The kids had to go everywhere with them. Alex told Tiff he was taking her to Canada for their honeymoon. Tiff bought all kinds of sexy nighties, body oils and anything that she thought might excite Alex. One day before the trip, Alex tells Tiff he is bringing his youngest daughter because the mother had a conference to attend. Tiff did not say anything but Oh God!

When Tiff and Alex go shopping, the kids had to come, the kids always asked their father to buy something for their mother. Every birthday party it was always Tiff and one of the ex-wives at the party. Tiff told herself after the kids finish high school maybe he would see her the way she wanted him too. It just did not happen; each day Tiff was getting weary. When it is a man's kids, the ex-wives do ugly things that the husband does not see because all he can see is keeping the peace. Alex was a good provider; in fact he was a workaholic. Both wives had affairs because he was so busy working, he just did not take the time to be the lover and provider the women need and wanted him to be.

Alex took Tiff on vacation every year but three or four kids had to go. Tiff was more like a nanny than a wife. One year Alex told Tiff he was taking her to Las Vegas, Tiff knew the kids could not go and she was so excited knowing finally her and Alex would be alone for fun. Tiff and Alex boarded the plane. Tiff in her big hat, new sun glasses, hair and nails done and all new pretty matching underwear and sexy nighties. Tiff was in her own world, what could go wrong. Alex took Tiff first class, not coach, food on glass plates with real silverware.

After Tiff and Alex got off the plane in Vegas, there was his oldest son Phillip, waiting at the airport, saying, daddy your flight was late. Tiff thought by Alex's son being twenty he would have gotten a room for him, instead he got a room with two beds. Tiff made up her mind she just could not go any farther. Tiff, a daughter of a preacher knew how to pray. Tiff was so desperate to leave Alex, she starts writing an ex-con. Tiff had to be celebrated at any cost. Tiff tried to talk to Alex but all he could see was she did not like his kids; she really did not, enough was enough. The last vacation Alex and Tiff took was to California, she did nothing special, and she knew he always had surprises for her.

They got off the plane and there were his two oldest sons. They got to California that Saturday, checked in the hotel and all of them went out to eat. Sunday was football day. Tiff told all her friends that she was going to see the New Orleans Saints play in California. Alex and his two sons went to the game; they left Tiff in the room to spend the whole day alone while Alex, her husband for 22 years and his 2 sons go to a professional football game. The best thing about being married to Alex, he indulged Tiff with stuff, but not himself. Alex taught Tiff how to do work that women were afraid to do, Tiff was a professional painter. Alex taught Tiff how to hang wallpaper and do all kinds of stuff.

Tiffany met Jerry online; they chatted and talked on the phone but mostly wrote each other. Everything Tiff needed to hear and wanted to hear Jerry was feeding her. Jerry spent 25 years in jail for killing a man behind a gold chain, Tiff had 23 years in a marriage that she was not happy in, and so what was the difference. Men from the joint can write all the right things and they can make their pencil write anything. Jerry told Tiff about his Christian experience, how he wanted to do ministry, how he wanted to work with young boys to keep them from living the life that he did and to teach them to stay away from crime, drugs and alcohol. One Saturday morning Tiff gets up after Alex goes to work, Tiff drove ten hours to be with Jerry the ex-con. Tiff stopped at every rest area drinking free cokes and orange juice. The scenes were very pretty; it was a good trip. Tiff stopped and laid in the grass and said to herself "Free at Last, Free at Last".

When Tiff got to Jerry, he was so sweet; his mother died and left him a house, as he was an only child. Tiff was disappointed in the house, Jerry did not have a dishwasher, how was Tiff going to wash dishes. Jerry did not have a washer or a dryer in the 21st century, which meant she had to go to the laundry mat like the common poor people. She had a problem going to the washer so Jerry washed the clothes. Finally, one day she went to the washer with Jerry, it was a good thing nobody knew her. She got enough courage to go by herself a few times. God had to break Tiff from her pride. After God broke Tiff, she befriended a woman from church. The woman thought it was awful that Tiff had to go to the Laundromat to wash. The woman's brother worked at Sears dent and bent, she had him to bring Tiff a washer and dryer. Jerry was so jealous and he was too mean to have it connected. Jerry was not serious about his walk with God.

Tiff stayed on Jerry about doing the right thing, Jerry told Tiff he did not think people really tried to live this Christian life. He never saw that before, he told Tiff that she was the first person he ever saw who tried to live a Christian life.

Tiff knew she had to do the right thing because she had left a husband after 23 years of marriage because she was bored, she knew that was not a reason for divorce. Tiff divorced Alex and married Jerry in a small chapel with a Notary. Tiff wanted to make this work; she asked Jerry let us pray together. Jerry told Tiff to pray for Tiff and Jerry would pray for Jerry. Tiff told Jerry "the Bible says a family that prays together will stay together."

Jerry was always so wrapped up in the sports station; he knew football players, their salary, their name and anything that came on the sports station day or night, Jerry watched it and knew it. Tiff starts seeing red flags. Jerry never read his Bible nor prayed and the ministry was a joke. Tiff was disappointed with Jerry, Tiff invested a lot in Jerry, and got so little from him, you would think after a woman has put her life on the line for a man he would show her some kind of appreciation.

However, the sad part was Jerry could not give what he did not know. Jerry never knew real love; he only knew game and what was published in books.

Wednesday night was Bible class night. Instead of Jerry taking Tiff to church, he told Tiff they were going to the club to eat free crabs, Tiff said Oh my god! Tiff prayed all day she even put holy oil on the suit she was wearing, she wore her black church suit, collar high around her neck, and her skirt was touching her toes. The minute Jerry and Tiff walked in the club the bartender asked Jerry why he brought Tiff to the club because she did not belong in a nightclub especially on a church night. Jerry told the bartender that Tiff was a Christian and her father was a preacher. The bartender gave Jerry a bag of Crabs and told Jerry to get Tiff out of there and never bring her back. Even though Tiff had problems with love, she still hung on to her faith. Jerry got busy trying to figure out a way to get rid of Tiff, he had her Bakers Acted, while her minister and a brother from the congregation stood on her front porch and watched. The police came and put handcuffs on her, the only thing she said to the police officer was she forgot her makeup, just in case they had cute guys in the nut house.

Tiff gets out of the police car, the police took the cuffs off Tiff, she walks in giving all her information, she looks around and she saw one man masturbating, one lady looking at the wall smiling, and one was catching flies. Tiff asked everybody to let us hold hands and pray. Tiff prayed herself out of there the same day.

Tiff knows how to pray herself out of any situation. When the doctor checked Tiff's blood pressure, it was two hundred; the doctor said they could not keep Tiff there because her pressure was too high, the secretary called different hospitals to see who would take Tiff. After checking different hospitals, the state told them to send Tiff to them.

The ambulance came and got Tiff, Tiff told the driver she was going in her own limousine. Tiff was so hurt but she was trying to hold her composure. When the ambulance brought Tiff to the hospital, the driver tried to explain to the nurse it was a case of a mean husband, but they just would not listen.

They put Tiff in a room with women who were in shackles, they had three police guards, guarding the door, and they had Tiff sitting in a recliner. Tiff did what she knew best to do and that was to pray.

Tiff had her hair fixed the day before and she got a manicure. The doctor came to Tiff asking Tiff when was the last time she did drugs. Tiff told the doctor she never used drugs. He asked Tiff when the last time she used alcohol. Tiff told the doctor she never used alcohol. He took Tiff's pressure and noticed it was two hundred, he asked Tiff if she took pressure pills. Tiff told him no. She told him all of this drama is the thing that ran her pressure up. They gave Tiff a pressure pill and Tiff prayed herself to sleep. When she woke up, the nurse came in the room and asked Tiff who she was visiting; Tiff told them she was one of them. A few minutes later, they came back and took Tiff's pressure again. Tiff's pressure was low; they told Tiff they had to send her back. Tiff pleaded with them not to send her back. Right before the ambulance got ready to take Tiff, her pressure had shot up again, they just could not send her back and they gave Tiff another pill. After an hour, God sent a woman doctor to Tiff's rescue, she sat down, talked to Tiff and asked Tiff what was really going on. Tiff broke down and told the doctor everything, the doctor told them to let Tiff go home because nothing was wrong with her. Jerry was so disappointed: yes, Tiff went right back to him. Jerry did not like that or the spunk that Tiff had.

One night Tiff and Jerry were arguing in bed. Tiff gets up goes in the kitchen; she did not turn on a light. She went to the silverware draw, opened it fast, closed it back very hard, and went back to bed. Jerry gets up and goes to sleep in another room; he thought Tiff had a knife. Jerry was 6ft. 3in., 220 pounds, but he was afraid of simple things. One Sunday, Tiff cooked some beef stew and Jerry ate and went to bed. When he woke up his tongue was white, Tiff told him he had mad-cow disease. Jerry dressed and flew straight to the emergency room; he told the nurse he had mad-cow disease. The nurse laughs at him; nobody in America ever had mad-cow disease.

Jerry was an aged man, he was ten years older than Tiff, but he was always bopping to secular music. He told Tiff he was still young at heart, Tiff told Jerry he was still worldly. Jerry went to work in New Orleans, La. after hurricane Katrina. Jerry was a sloppy worker; after he made a few dollars, he tried to get in a gated neighborhood and could not because he was an ex-con, which is why the neighborhood was gated to keep his kind out. Jerry came back home so angry because the people in New Orleans treated him the way he was, a sloppy ex-con with a bad attitude.

By Tiff being flip at the lips she tells Jerry "it is what it is". He was so angry he struck Tiff, yes, she was surprised; she saw stars and the moon. She looked at Jerry and said I got a real man because men strike their wives but punks walk away. Jerry was so angry he slept in the chair. Jerry was so angry with Jerry. Jerry told Tiff one day he was going to kill her. Tiff loved to quote the scriptures, she told Jerry for Tiff to live is Christ, but to die is gain, but it was best for him to let her live, because if he touched her, he would end up in hell, by way of jail. Tiff told Jerry she does not fear the man who can destroy her body but she fears the man who can destroy both body and soul.

Jerry looked at Tiff one night and told her he do not know how to love her, he prayed that God would teach him how to love her. Tiff looked at Jerry and said all you have to do is read the word. It will teach you how to love your wife and not be bitter toward her, Tiff told him it is all in the word. Tiff had no more respect for Jerry. Jerry asked if their minister could talk to them, Tiff said sure why not. When their minister came over, he told Jerry his thinking was so wrong by trying to make Tiff look bad. Jerry told the minister that Tiff does not like men, she just likes the sex.

The minister did not respond, he just looked at Tiff under eye. Jerry did not know that the minister knew many men who would enjoy a woman like Tiff. He set Tiff up real good. The minister was so out done he did not even think to pray, Tiff had to ask for prayer. Jerry knew the street games, but Tiff knew the church game.

Jerry stopped making love to Tiff six months before he put her out, he did not know it, but he was getting her ready for single life. Tiff prayed every day, saying Lord, get me out of here and he did. Jerry thought it was him. Tiff and Jerry went to church on Father's Day. After church, Tiff cooked a full meal, Jerry ate his dinner then left and went to the old timers dance in the park. Tiff went back to night service. Every night before Tiff goes to bed, she would read her Bible with her friend from Louisiana, and they would pray. After prayer, Tiff crawled in bed behind Jerry. Tiff slept like a log that night. Jerry woke Tiff up at 6 a.m. the next day telling Tiff he just cannot do her anymore, he wanted her to leave; he also told Tiff he would bring her to work, Tiff looks at Jerry and says thanks but no thanks because she didn't want him in her head. Jerry had no job; his sloppy business folded up and he stopped getting calls.

Tiff was paying all the bills. They had two vehicles but Jerry was so mean trying to hurt her, he kept both vehicles. While she showered she sang all of her freedom songs. Tiff put a washcloth, make-up, soap and deodorant in her purse, picked up her umbrella and told Jerry she'll see him at noon when she come to get her clothes.

Tiff walked to work the hot sun beaming down on her. Tiff talked to God, she repented for everything she ever done wrong. Tiff was the first person at work, she shared with her co-worker that she was homeless; everybody said, we would take you but we do not have the space. They asked her what she was going to do. Tiff panicked a little, not being from the city and she did not know many people but Tiff knew how to pray. Tiff remembered the old man who said he was turning his shed into an apartment. Tiff got the phone book and looked up Mr. Hawthorne's number. Tiff gave him a call. Tiff inquired about the apartment. Mr. Hawthorne said he had not put air in the place. Tiff said it was ok, he asked Tiff when she needed the apartment, she told him today at noon, he told her to come on. Tiff hung up and said thank you sweet Jesus, this was Florida in June, but Tiff did not want to be on the streets.

Tiff borrowed a truck, went to Jerry's place to get her stuff. Jerry thought because he told Tiff he wanted her out that same day, that she was going to kiss his butt, crying telling him she had nobody, and nowhere to go, asking him could she stay until she found a place, trying to break her spirit. However, he forgot, Tiff knew how to pray and she was cute. The only thing Jerry would let Tiff get was her clothes and that was cool with Tiff. Jerry was fussing saying she was moving too slow and taking too long. Tiff looked at Jerry and said, if she knew last night she had to move, she would have start packing then.

Jerry told Tiff that is why he was putting her out because she was too smart. However, he only told her that morning, she suggested to Jerry if she was moving too slow he could help her. Jerry starts throwing Tiff stuff on the truck. Jerry got a phone call while Tiff was there, he referred to her as his ex-wife, Tiff just played it off as if she did not hear Jerry. After Tiff finished packing, Jerry asked for his ring back, Tiff took off her wedding band and gave it back to Jerry. As Tiff was leaving, she stretched her arms out, asking Jerry for a hug; she told him she was so sorry she disappointed him. Tiff walked out with her dignity.

The best thing about being married to Jerry, he put her out.

When Tiff got to Mr. Hawthorne's house, he met her. Mr. Hawthorne was in his late 80's, and he has a 12-year-old son. Mr. Hawthorne told Tiff that he had a two-bedroom apartment, the tenant left last night, but he did not have time to clean the place. He said the rent was six hundred and fifty dollars a month, Tiff said she wanted it. The apartment was semi furnished; all Tiff needed was a place to lay her head. The place had a washer and dryer but no dishwasher. Tiff figured she could always buy paper plates. In Tiff's mind, she was saying look at God. Tiff dumped all her stuff in the middle of the bed took a shower went back to work. After work, Tiff kept the truck and went on to school. Tiff told her instructor what happened, he said "and you still came to class". After class, Tiff went to one of her church members home, who has been Tiff's mother every since she came to Florida. Tiff borrowed two sheets and a pillowcase. When Tiff told her what happened, she did not believe Tiff because she was not crying. Tiff went to her new home, dumped everything on the floor, put her two sheets on her bed and prayed herself to sleep, thanking God that she was not homeless.

Three days later Jerry calls Tiff's job saying he made a mistake by putting her out and he still loves her and asked her to please come back home. Tiff told Jerry he had the wrong number. Whoever he was looking for did not work there anymore.

Reality kicked in, Jerry realized he had no income and no body to pay the bills; that is why his love kicked in.

Jerry did not know that Tiff had bought a six hundred dollar car from an auction. Tiff knew the marriage was going down and she knew she would need transportation. All she had to do was buy her license plate.

Jerry called Tiff one day and invited her to come eat bar-b-que with him. Tiff told Jerry she does not hang out with the enemy. Another time Jerry saw Tiff at church and asked could he talk with her, Tiff answer was nope I do not have time. He looked at Tiff with her short skirt and had the nerve to tell her it was too short, she looked at Jerry as if he was a piece of crap.

Tiff put in for her divorce; Jerry tried to stop it, telling the Judge how much he still loved her, The Judge asked Tiff if she was willing to try another six month, Tiff told the judge she didn't want to try six more seconds.

Tiff told the judge he was not the man she thought he was, and she just could not do it. Tiff said to herself, another bad mistake.

Tiff was put out in June. In November, Tiff met an ex-football player, Spencer, who called the office, he was looking for Mr. Johnson, her manager. When Mr. Johnson came back to the office, Tiff gave him the message. Spencer, a retired professional football player was collecting donations for black football teams in the hood. Mr. Johnson asked Tiff to call Spencer back and tell him to get the donations from the people he buys his insurance from. Mr. Johnson did not realize the call came from Dallas. Spencer told Tiff she had a sexy voice, which she already knew, he asked if he could call her back sometimes, she said ok.

They talked and talked on the phone. Tiff told Spencer about the drama she was going through. Spencer sent a picture of himself; Tiff emailed her picture also. When Spencer saw Tiff's smile, he had the Florist send a long stem rose to her every day until Christmas. Tiff felt cute, special, and sexy again.

Tiffany said to herself, Spencer recognizes beauty just from a photo and phone voice. Tiffany talked with Spencer day and night.

Tiff loved the attention. Spencer asked Tiff to come to Dallas for Thanksgiving, Tiff told him she had obligated herself to work the homeless shelter. Tiff had fun working the homeless shelter; all eyes would be on her. She was the center of attention.

Spencer continues to send flowers to her. Spencer asked Tiff what she liked and disliked in a man. Tiff made it clear she did not want a man that drank, smoked, nor do drugs because she enjoys kissing and when you kiss a man with alcohol or any kind of drugs on his breath he smells like burnt trees.

Spencer made plans to visit with Tiff at Christmas; he made a reservation to stay at the Regency Hotel. Tiff spends a whole day getting ready for his visit. She was at the salon from 8 a.m. until 7 p.m. Tiff had her nails and hair done, a foot massage, the whole nine yards. Tiff shopped making sure she had at least five matching under garments.

Tiff met Spencer at the airport; he was wearing blue jeans, a suede jacket, had a baldhead, with a cowboy hat and cowboy boots. Spencer was 6ft 4in. Tiff was wondering what he was packing. Spencer had big hands and wore a size 13 shoe.

Tiff wondered what I am about to get. Spencer kissed Tiff and she knew then he had lied because when he kissed her, it made her so sick. She asked Spencer what time the next flight leaves because she could not do him. He said they did not have to kiss, she told him looking sad, kissing is part of lovemaking, without kissing it was just sex. She was upset and she asked Spencer what else he lied about. Spencer dips snuff and smoke cigars. Tiff left Spencer at the airport. Spencer called Tiff and told her she was the definition of a bitch. He had traveled this far to be with her and she is acting like this. Tiff let Spencer know that she hates a liar; she told Spencer all liars have their part in the lake of fire. The best thing about Spencer, he gave Tiff her self-esteem back.

Tiff spends Christmas and New Year alone because she had to hang on to her integrity.

The month of March, Tiff was in the store shopping for groceries, which is when she met Chris. Chris was 5ft 8in tall, pretty smile and he was a body builder. Chris asked Tiff for her phone number, Tiff did not know her number because she lives alone and never calls herself. Chris owns his own trucking company and he had two 18-wheelers. Chris owns a jeep and a small pickup.

Chris passed the office where Tiff worked and got her number off the billboard. He gave her a call a week later; he had to tell her who he was because Tiff is so cute, she meets guys all the time. Chris let Tiff know he was interested in her and Tiff let Chris know that she was ten years older than he was. Chris tells Tiff the thing that validates a man is his walk with God. That sounds good to Tiff. Chris was very interesting after talking on the phone a month. Chris came to Tiff's job for an insurance quote on his truck. He gave her his information and she assured him she would work up some good numbers for him.

A month later, Chris calls Tiff for a date, she agrees. Chris let her know that he wanted to spend time with her, but it had to be early evening or late night. Tiff agrees for early evening. Tiff had to spend Friday night from 4:30 until closing to enhance her cuteness. Tiff wore her short gray and red button down dress so Chris could see her cleavage and her legs. Tiff left the top button unbuttoned, hoping Chris would notice. Tiff also wore her red pumps and red accessories. Chris picked Tiff up and told her she looked nice. To Tiff, nice was not enough, she wanted to hear "she looked stunning".

Chris was well groomed, he had on a starched ironed shirt; he washed his jeep for the occasion.

Chris takes Tiff to a nice restaurant. Chris apologizes and tells Tiff he taught a drug class at 6:00 p.m. that same evening, he had to call and encourage the people to come. Every time Chris made a call, it made Tiff feel so good because she sees that this man really does care about people. Tiff thought to herself "I could do him".

Chris told Tiff that he was a very busy man. He was over the drug ministry, the prison ministry, and the hospital and nursing home. Tiff was very impressed; she finally found just what she wanted. Tiff asked Chris if she could go with him to the drug class. Chris looked at Tiff and said yes, sure, most time when I tell women I am a minister they go the other way. Tiff got very religious; she told Chris only what you do for Christ will last.
Chris and Tiff ministered in the park one Saturday. There were many homeless people there; people that ordinary folks did not care to be around. The other church folk was just standing together as if their life was in danger. Tiffany maneuvered her way through the crowd telling the people there is a better life, a better way.

Give God a chance. After the person said they wanted to try God, Tiff would lead them to Chris knowing he would tell them the right thing. Tiff forgot about how cute she was, she was in her glory; they led about 20 souls to Christ. Tiff led souls to Chris. After that service, he asked her, why did she bring everybody that accepted Christ to him instead of bringing the souls to some of the other ministers that were out there, Tiff told Chris she was out there with him.

Tiff girlfriend from Louisiana spent her vacation with Tiff. Tiff had her taking pictures just for Chris. You would have thought Tiff was Chris wife, whatever it took to make Chris look good that is what Tiff did.

Chris brought Tiff home that same night after ministering. Mr. Hawthorne was looking out the window, he noticed Chris bringing Tiff home, and he was so upset. The next day he gave Tiff three days to move. Tiff told him she was moving but not in three days. He told Tiff he was going to put her stuff on the street. Tiff told him she knew the law also and she had to have thirty days and a good reason. Tiff goes back in her little house, fell on her knees, and told God I am right back in the same predicament I was in six months ago.

Tiff stayed on her knees waiting for an answer from the Lord. The Lord led her to an elderly man and his wife who attends their congregation. Tiff told them what happened and they had an empty small two-bedroom house, they told Tiff that she could rent but it had to be painted. Tiff told them she knew how to paint. Tiff called Chris and told him what happened. Chris being a man of God, asked Tiff if she wanted him to go talk to Tiff's land lord, Tiff told him no because God had blessed her with another place. He asked Tiff how did that happen so fast. She told him she got God's attention.

Tiff goes to church the next day, when she gets home from church, Mr. Hawthorne had put a poem and a long stem rose on her front door. If he wanted her like that, why did he charge her six hundred and fifty dollars? If Tiff knew it was like that, she would have given him fifty dollars and a promise. Tiff read the poem, got angry, and threw it in the trash. He was like Jerry; he knew she had nothing and nowhere to go. He thought she would kiss his butt in spite of it all.
She has a God who really sees her. Chris helped Tiff move and fix up her little house; Tiff called her house her little green acre house. Chris and Tiff ministered at the senior citizens homes; he preached and she sang.

Some people thought Tiff could not sing but she would try anything for Chris. Sometimes, Chris would be late and Tiff would be there by herself, instead of Tiff waiting for Chris she would walk around and ask the seniors what song had been ringing down in them that week. Whatever song they came up with Tiff would try to sing. There were times when Chris would look at Tiff and tell her she was so wonderful. Tiff knew Chris two favorite songs; every time before Chris preached Tiff had to sing just for him he would look at her and smile. During the time, Chris was preaching, Tiff had to say Amen and stand up and clap for her man.

As soon as he finished, Tiff had to sing his other song. Nobody could tell Tiff that was not how the song went. Tiff just felt in her heart whenever, wherever Chris preached Tiff had to be there pushing and encouraging him. Tiff being old school, it bothered her when she rode with Chris and he was playing Jazz on the radio. Tiff knew Chris had a unique ministry. Tiff felt that if a drug user called Chris, nine times out of ten he or she was in trouble. Tiff felt Chris should keep a praying spirit because the word of God says men should always pray. The scripture talked about having the mind of Christ.

Tiff was so proud of Chris, when Chris told Tiff he needed time to be away from her to hear from God, poor Tiff believed him; she just stayed home and prayed for him. Tiff thought there was no man under the sun like Chris. When Tiff thought about it, the relationship was his ministry. Chris drove an eighteen- wheeler, some time he would leave out at midnight sometimes later and call for Tiff to pray with him, Tiff would try to call down heaven for Chris, she would pray so hard until she got God's attention for Chris.

Another time Chris was praying as he was driving alone; God would drop scriptures in Chris Spirit. He would call Tiff and ask her to get the Bible and read different scriptures for him. Tiff wouldn't be in the spirit, she always tried to read soft and low in her finest voice. Chris would tell her she would have to read louder because the truck made so much noise. There were times when Chris would let Tiff ride in the truck with him. Tiff brought all kinds of religious books and she had one with questions from every book in the Bible.
The most precious thing Chris ever said to Tiff was, he covers her every day, meaning he talked to God on her behalf. Chris had to speak for the Evangelist team in an apartment complex, Tiff thinking she could sing, always did praise, and worship; she

would pray all night and God always moved in the service. Anyway, Tiff got there ten minutes before Chris. Chris pulls up driving another woman's car. Chris gets out, go around, open the door for her, and bring her in on his arms. Thank God for the all night prayer Tiff had. Chris had the nerve to bring another woman to service, and he embraced Tiff. Tiff asked him how could he; his response was "its only church". Tiff said no more. Tiff said to herself she just could not believe him, how could he when he always told her how wonderful she was and that she was the thing that had been missing In his life, Tiff saw so much in Chris. Tiff was hurt so bad, she was fighting back the tears. She sat there and asked God to please give her the strength she needed. Tiff did not know whether to clown with an open confrontation; she did not know whether to leave, or to go on with the service.

By Tiff being a preacher's daughter, she went on with the service. She had to forget about herself and that's when she did a service unto God and not Chris because she knew then, that Chris really didn't give a damn about her. That was the last time Chris and Tiff did anything together. Chris was still trying to play her stupid, weak, or crazy.

He couldn't understand why he and Tiff couldn't still do ministry together and why the two of them couldn't be friends while him and his new lover was being together all over the place. Chris has a large family, half of them in church but the other half is waiting on him. Chris family has seen so much corruption and they just moved away from church. Tiff and Chris family always prayed that one day Chris would walk in his calling. Tiff told Chris that God said he was going to bless her with enough income that she could work and support the two of them while he ministered full time and Tiff would go with him sometimes at night and on weekends.

One year later, Chris comes back to Tiff telling her he made a mistake and that he will always love her and he knows she still loves him. There is nobody else like Tiff, she knows all that; nobody is as fine and cute, and sexy who can be everything that God and Chris wanted. When Chris pulled the rug out from under Tiff, she fell so hard. Tiff is still pulling splinters out of her butt.

What Tiff got from Chris, she learned how to do street ministry without being afraid. Tiff just went on being Tiff. She could not figure out the problem, she did a reality check on herself. She went to the word; the word told her she was better than blessed.

The word told her she was more than a conqueror, the word told her she was royal and a princess.

Tiff has pretty big brown eyes, dimples, pretty white teeth, nice bust, small waste line, big hips, nice size butt, and a sexy voice. When Tiff passed her mirror, the mirror says cute. 99% of the time she is right, she is just downright pretty.

Tiff concluded that black men just could not handle all of that in one black woman. When the relationships are over and it hits them, the first thing they say My! My! My! What a fool I was to let her go. Tiff just knew she was what the men needed and wanted. Tiff was a good catch, but she just could not hold a man because all she was looking for was someone to love Tiff the way she deserved to be loved. Tiff was a flirt but not much of that. Once a man got to know Tiff, they saw she meant Jesus every step of the way. Tiff woke up Saturday morning and said to herself she was going to her old church on Sunday. Saturday, Tiff spent the day in the salon, getting a manicure, pedicure, massage, and her hair done, Tiff shopped for a new suit and shoes. Tiff walked in church Sunday morning late because she knew all eyes would turn and look at her as she walks down the aisle.

Tiff wanted everybody to see her new navy blue suit and powder blue matching camisole and her navy and powder blue shoes. She sat on the second pew. After the second song, the usher brought Tiff a note that read, "Would you have dinner with me today"? Tiff looked up from reading the note, this preacher sitting on the high seat had this big smile looking at Tiff, letting her know that the note was from him. The song leader asked everybody to show some love. Rev. Bartley made his way to Tiff and introduced himself, telling Tiff how nice she looked. Tiff was eating it up because she already knew how good she was looking.

The service was good and the sermon was "You have not, because you asked not". Rev. Bartley ate the sermon up. After the sermon, the pastor asked Rev. Bartley to have words; he was tall, average looking, he wore a navy blue suit and navy alligator shoes. He spoke well. After service, Rev. Bartley went straight to Tiff trying to usher her out before she could talk to anybody else.

He took Tiff to a buffet restaurant, Tiff noticed Rev. Bartley knew some word. As they were eating and talking, a lady came in the restaurant with her two small children, she was expecting a third baby.

Rev. Bartley stopped the lady and asked her had anyone prayed for her since she is expecting. She said no in her soft shy voice. Rev. Bartley asked her if she minded him praying for her and her baby, she said no. Rev. Bartley let the lady and her children get their food, as he and Tiff talked. Tiff told Rev. Bartley she had attended Bible College. The conversation went well.

After Tiff had eaten all she could eat, Rev. Bartley asked her to come on lets go pray for the lady. Rev. Bartley begins to pray for the young lady, he asked Tiff to lay her hands on the young lady's stomach. The young lady began to cry, he prayed for the other children. After he finished praying for the lady, Tiff asked her if she was having a boy the lady said yes. You could not tell Tiff she was not a prophetess, and a healer. After that, every time you saw Tiff she had on her long white dress, and long sleeves. Another time Tiff and Rev. Bartley went to Wal-Mart and this young girl with her baby was walking down the aisle. All Rev. Bartley said was good evening young lady, she just broke down and started crying. Tiff hugged the young lady and Rev. Bartley began to pray. She said it was so hard, she was thinking about killing herself and her baby.

Tiff preached to the lady telling her "God puts no more on you than you can bear", and that her baby was a blessing. Rev. Bartley gave her twenty dollars and she began to smile.

Rev. Bartley told Tiff that maybe their calling is to minister to young hurting women. Rev. Bartley and Tiff would be on the phone until late hours at night talking about the word. He could read Greek and Hebrew. He used to wash Tiff with the word of God day and night. He never got out of the way with her. Tiff knew this was a man of God. She encouraged him to have Bible study in his home every Wednesday night, and they did. Tiff invited her friends and their friends invited their friends, there were up to twenty people. Tiff told them the man of God was teaching God's word, and he was. Things were going good; some nights he and Tiff would be on the phone until after midnight talking about the word of God. That was just their life. Tiff and Rev. Bartley was talking about getting a building because of the over flow. One Wednesday, Tiff was late for Bible class and saw this strange woman in the kitchen, she looked about Tiff's age. Tiff began to wonder, who is this making their refreshments. Tiff was cool but she could not get home fast enough to call Rev. Bartley and ask him who was the lady.

He said that was his ex-wife, they had been divorced for fifteen years. Tiff asked him why she was so interested in hearing him now. Rev. Bartley tells Tiff his ex has a soul. Tiff said let us strengthen the link that we have and once we get a building, any and every body can come. She also suggested to Rev. Bartley, since he wasn't working why couldn't he have Bible class one night a week for his family and another night with Tiff and her friends. Rev. Bartley said you are just being jealous. Every Wednesday night after class, Tiff and her girls would go to her house to talk about how they could enhance the class.

This Wednesday night was different. Tiff's girls were ready to blast him and quit the class. Tiff was trying to convince them that there was no danger in the water. Sister Martha said she did not like it. Sister James said she was a prophetess and God is showing her there is a fly in the milk. Tiff calmed them all down and said let us just ride it out, if it is not real the Lord will reveal it to us. The class is going so well and if they don't stand firm the devil will destroy it. A month passed and everything was going well, the ex did not come any more. She just wanted to see what Tiff looked like because Rev. Bartley had been running his mouth about Tiff.

Nobody missed a class because the class was good. Tiff and her girls showed up at the same time as usual, when a skinny female crack head answered the door. Tiff and her girls were smoking, Tiff asked them to please, please be cool. The class was awful, as soon as Tiff prayed the dismissal prayer they got out of there. They did not care for talking, refreshments, or fellowship. They all went back to Tiff's house. The sisters' start saying, we told you he was not any good, the devil knows the word too, everybody jumped all over Tiff. Tiff sat there and said nothing.

Rev. Bartley called Tiff twenty times she never answered the phone, she just said, "Why me Lord". Five a.m. Thursday morning Rev. Bartley knocked and knocked pleading for Tiff to open the door, Tiff opened the door, as if she did not have a clue that he was knocking, he asked her to listen, and she still did not say a word. He told Tiff that was an ex-girl friend who had nowhere to go and she asked him if she could stay until she found a place, she is not working at this time. The preacher asked Tiff did she hear him, Tiff said no. Rev. Bartley told Tiff he was seeking God as to which one of them would make him the best first lady, the ex-wife for fifteen-year, the crack head, or Tiff. Tiff prayed very hard and quick for the right answer, she looked at Rev. Bartley and said, she would love to help him and God. He could take Tiff out of the race and out of his equation.

Tiff called her girls and asked them to come over at nine that same morning. The prophetess, the mother, and the missionary, jumped on her. Saying they knew he was nothing to start with. They told her never ever invite them to another Bible Class with her man of God. Tiff just sat and listened. After her friends finished dogging her out, it finally dawned on them why Tiff invited them over.

Tiff's friends start dogging all men out saying they are so selfish, so rude, so into themselves. It is so sad how men let a little tail get them side tracked. When Tiff finally spoke, she said it was a spirit, a sprit that put blinders on the men of God. Tiff believes it came from not having a personal relationship with God; we are not going back, let us just pray for him. Sister Mary said pray like hell, let us just put him in hell, let's just kill him and cut him up and feed him to the dogs. When Tiff finally told them about the decision, he was trying to make, they started all over again, saying "and you did not go off on him". Tiff said she just could not stoop that low; for him to even wonder about the crack head, he had to be still using.

That night was the end of the bible class. He realized his mistake; he thought he was going to still have the class. Three months later, he asked Tiff to please come back and help.

What Tiff got from Rev. Bartley is because a man can quote scripture, it does not mean he is saved.

Tiff called her best friend Vanessa in Louisiana. Vanessa is married to a white guy. Tiff tells Vanessa she just cannot do brothers anymore, she is steady pouring out and they are playing games. She tells Vanessa she is thinking about changing over; she just cannot do brothers anymore. Vanessa pleads with Tiff not to change over, Tiff asks why? Vanessa reminds Tiff she was born in Alabama and raised in Mississippi. If Tiff married a white guy and she made him angry, Tiff would probably have flash backs thinking he had it twisted and thought he was talking to one of his slaves and that would not be too nice for him. Vanessa told Tiff the white guy she gets involved with, when mad day came and it will, you would make the white guy pay for everything the slave owner ever done. Vanessa pleaded with Tiff to stay with the brothers. Tiff decided she just was not relationship material; she parked her car and caught the city bus for eight month going to nursing school. Tiff not caring about anything nor any body, she did not worry about make-up; she only wore her uniforms to school. The young guys on the bus flirted with Tiff. One guy brought Tiff lunch every day, they sat together on the bus, but they never really got together. Tiff riding the bus, what does she need with a man who's also riding the bus. He brought Tiff good lunches. He even caught the bus and visited Tiff church several times.

Tiff was trying to stay on the straight and narrow, not dating for a whole year. All Tiff did was work, school and church just enjoying life. Tiff met this giant from Kingsley, Jamaica. He was six feet nine inches tall; he told Tiff he was from Ethiopia; all of his front teeth are missing. He told Tiff she was his kind of woman. Tiff said the hell I am, I do not want to get gumdrops (kissing without teeth) when I kiss. His children's mother was living in a homeless shelter, the kids were in foster care, and he was trying to get someone to help him get his children. Tiff ran real fast because she could not deal with more little children.

Chapter 4
Gavin, God Sent

One Saturday morning and it happened on a Saturday. I mean the first Saturday of the month, the first Saturday in October, the weather was just a little cool, no clouds in the sky. Tiff took the city bus to work, no makeup, and no jewelry. Tiff was wearing a red hair do and has pretty white teeth and always a warm smile.

Tiff was sitting at her desk, this drop dead gorgeous black man and his daughter was standing in front of Tiff's desk, Tiff looked up, she wonder was she in heaven or what, She asked the man if she could help him, and he smiled, oh my God! What a smile, the man had sexy bedroom eyes, pretty smile, white teeth, meaning he did not smoke, a nice voice. His mustache was pretty wild needing a shave just enough to look a little rugged, hair thinning on the top, salt and pepper hair, he is not tall. He reminds Tiff of Zacchaeus in the Bible, Zacchaeus was a short man in stature but smart. Zacchaeus was the tax collector, so he had plenty money, some of yours and mine and he promised to give back. Gavin does not look over confident; he seems like a take-charge man.

The man made sure Tiff knew that was his daughter even though he did not have on a wedding band, Tiff said to herself, maybe he does yard work or some kind of work where his ring might get dirty or damaged. Tiff was looking for the light band where he had been wearing a wedding band. He told Tiff about his business. His name was Gavin; he was not chocolate brown, maybe mocha.

Gavin told Tiff he had three businesses. Tiff was thinking to herself, she could be his fourth business or she could be his private secretary. The first thing crossed Tiff's mind, he has a wife, money and he keeps the little girl with him for protection. Tiff remembered she had no makeup or jewelry, was trying to flirt with this cute sexy man.

Tiff told Gavin about the business she was trying to start. He said nothing as if he was not paying her any attention. Gavin goes in his wallet to give Tiff one of his business cards. Tiff noticed his small hands, smooth like he never done a day's work in his life. He asked Tiff for her number, she gave it to him. She was so excited for a split second knowing he was not going to call. As he walked away from Tiff's desk, Tiff noticed his fine round sexy butt. Tiff said to herself, I could do him.

That was the first time Tiff ever laid eyes on Gavin, Tiff thought to herself, he is sexy, cute, sweet smile, nice butt and married.

Tiff finally got it together; he is only a man, a black man with a wife. So take your hungry looking eyes off him. As the day passed she never thought of him again. Tiff got off work went to a little country town where Vanessa's son was preaching, the service was good. Tiff spent time with Cardel, Vanessa's son. Cardel has been preaching since he was three years old, Cardel use to stand on a box because he was so short; after Sunday's and Wednesday's service Vanessa and Tiff would stay over after church to shout for Cardel and give him all the moral support he needed. Cardel was very smart, he was the drum major in high school, he also got his Masters of Divinity. Cardel thought whenever he preached close to his nanny Tiff, she was supposed to be there. Tiff promised Cardel she would come back Sunday. Tiff had someone drop her off at the little country service, she realized that she left her cell phone home. When Tiff returned home; she saw this strange number on her cell phone. She dialed it back and it was Gavin. Tiff said, "Oh my God, this is him". Tiff could not stop smiling. The name did not stick with Tiff but the smile, dreamy eyes and sexy butt did.

Gavin asked how was her day, Tiff told Gavin it could not get any better. He asked Tiff had she eaten, he asked her if she liked Chinese food, Tiff said yes, he told Tiff he would be there to pick her up in 30 minutes. Tiff was so excited; she started to wonder what would she wear. Should she wear what she wore to church, should she put on jeans, or should she wear shorts, she wore her tight fitting jeans. Tiff really could not believe this was happening to her.

This fine sexy, pretty smile, cute little butt man was coming to Tiff's house, in the hood. Tiff lived next door to a drug dealer and across the street lives another drug dealer. However, nobody messed with Tiff or her belongings, they all called Tiff the church lady. One day Tiff was talking to her neighbors and asked, if she put a sign in her yard that said drugs for sale, would she get any business? Tiff's neighbors told Tiff to stick with the church because that is not the way it's done. Tiff asked do you run an ad in the newspaper; they laugh and told Tiff you do not do it like that, but if she did, she probably would not get caught, because the police would think it was a joke because nobody is that stupid. Tiff lived in the hood but she was not a hood rat.

Gavin arrives thirty minutes later, he pulls in front of the door, driving his SUV as she was coming out of her house. Gavin gets out to open the door for her, Tiff felt like a princess. Gavin asked her how was church, Tiff told Gavin all about the sermon, and he just listens patiently. The restaurant was less than half a mile from the house. Gavin ordered shrimp fried rice and so did Tiff. Neither one of them ate their food, they just picked over it.

Tiff told Gavin about the business she wanted to start which is a senior living facility. She told him she wants to buy a prefab four bedroom home, that way she could take three bedrooms for the business and she used the master bed room for her living quarters. Tiff thought $63,000 was a steal. Gavin asked her why she wanted to spend so much when she could get the same thing for less money with no mortgage. Gavin said you could do the same thing for twenty thousand dollars or less. He mentioned that she could open three centers for the price she wanted to pay for one. Tiff thought to herself "he must be a genius". You could not tell her that Gavin was not God sent. Gavin being such a wonderful, sweet, precious, thoughtful, and kind man. When he left Tiff Saturday, he and his realtor got together and began looking for Tiff a house. Tiff knew if you take care of God's business, he would take care of yours. You could not tell Tiff that Gavin was not God sent. Gavin asked Tiff if she felt like taking a ride, she answered why not, anything to keep from going home; Gavin was all business. What made Tiff feel so special? This man was looking out for her. No man she ever dated went that far out of the way for her. Gavin and Tiff was not dating. Gavin had gone far enough to print houses off the internet that his realtor sent him. Gavin used his ink, paper, time, and gas. One house had a big yard, a closed in porch. It was nice but needed a lot of work that Tiff knew she was not about to do. She had just met Gavin and no way could she expect him to do the work. She was slowly getting the picture; the next house Gavin showed her was a nice brick with gray stone on the front. Tiff fell in love with that house. As Gavin showed the houses, she began to let herself go and really trust this man. Tiff mentioned she had an appointment with the prefab man on Tuesday, Gavin said ok, she was convinced his way was the best way, so she cancelled her appointment.

Just think about it, when God drops something or somebody out of the sky to help you, to drive you all over town in his

SUV, gives his time, patience, and gas, you do not second-guess it. You know it is God. Tiff told Gavin she wanted him to check on the stone and brick house for her. She was going to trust his judgment because she knew since he was this interested he would find her the right place.

Tiff has a friend who lives in a small city; he asked Tiff if she would paint three rooms in his house. She spent all day Tuesday trying to help this young minister with his house. Tiff was doing something nice for somebody else while Gavin and the realtor were looking out for her. Tiff does not care what it is you just cannot beat God giving. Gavin called Tiff to ask her to meet them, as bad as Tiff wanted the house she asked Gavin to wait until the next day. Tiff felt so good knowing somebody was behind the scene working it out for her. Tiff worked the whole day; she was tired she did not call Gavin until the next day. Tiff went to bed that night thanking God for putting such a man in her life.
The next day we looked at the stone and brick house, but it was already under contract; Gavin showed her three more houses. After looking at all the houses, she asked Gavin which one did he like the best, Gavin said for the plans that you have made, you need four bed rooms.

The one she bought would be the best one. Gavin has a way of making decisions for Tiff but making she feels that she made the decision herself. I guess he learned that from his sisters. Tiff chose the house she wanted. Gavin arranged for the realtor to meet with them to show the house inside and out. The house is a four bedroom with two new baths, new windows, a new kitchen sink, and cabinets. Gavin looked at Tiff and asked Tiff how do she plan to pay for the house? He explained to Tiff when you buy a bank foreclosure you have to pay cash. Tiff looked at Gavin and said my heavenly father is rich. Tiff went home, made a couple phone calls, got someone to believe in her dream, and let Tiff have the money. The bank was asking for twenty-two thousand nine hundred dollars. Tiff asked Gavin how much to offer the bank? He told her to offer sixteen thousand. Tiff told Gavin that was too low, the realtor also thought like Tiff that was too low; Gavin gave Tiff that real serious look and looked away, Tiff told the realtor sixteen thousand. The realtor told Tiff she had to show that she had sixteen thousand in the bank, Tiff had it all in one day except 200.00, she borrowed the two hundred from her pastor until the bank wrote the letter, and then she took the money back to her pastor.

Every session that Tiff had with the realtor, she thought Gavin had to go with her. Gavin was so kind, he walked her through it. Tiff wondered what kind of man is this. As Tiff mentioned to her friends how nice Gavin was, they always asked is he white? Tiff would say nope this is a brother with his head on straight. Then the day came to close on the house. Tiff needed five hundred dollars, which she mentions to Gavin. He gives it to her as if it was only five dollars. Gavin knew Tiff less than three weeks and give it to Tiff. Tiff said to herself, I am going to make this man mine. When a man gives a woman that much money, not knowing if she is a man or woman, yes that is God sent.

When Tiff and Gavin went to the bank to get the cashier check to close on the house, two people referred to Gavin as Tiff's husband. Tiff was dressed as if she was going to church all suited down in a navy blue suit with matching shoes. Gavin wore navy slacks and a blue and yellow shirt, looking good enough to eat with that sweet sexy smile.

After Tiff closed on the house deal, Gavin looked at her, shook her hand, and told her his job was finished, good luck, she will not be needing his service any more.

Tiff was fighting back the tears. There was no way Tiff was going to let this wonderful man go. Tiff wanted Gavin to go with her to christen the house together but Gavin told her to let her man christen the house with her. Tiff said in her low teary voice, Gavin you are my man. He did not respond.

Tiff was excited about her four-bed room two-bath house. Tiff had her keys in her hand, but she was still a little sad, because she would not see Gavin anymore. Tiff had to think of a way to stay in Gavin's life, so the day after Tiff closed, she called Gavin about four times and he would not pick up the phone.

Tiff had to think very hard how to keep this man, Gavin had never tried to kiss Tiff; he never gave Tiff false hope. She told Gavin one day that she was his girl friend. Gavin told her that is what you say. Tiff said to herself "she had to have this man". Gavin was not married; he was a single, young black professional businessman. Tiff wondered if it was the age difference because Tiff was older than Gavin, but he was more mature business wise. Tiff thought about how she had nothing to bring to the table. Tiff could not think of anything to say or do to impress Gavin.

After thinking, Tiff remembered Gavin had mentioned to her that she should buy three houses and have three group homes. Tiff reminded Gavin of that and his job was not over until the third house was purchased.

Tiff made up her mind that she was not going to sweat Gavin about having a personal relationship, and will settle at being business partners and good friends. A few days after she settled in her spirit of being friends and business partners, she said, God you know I want so much more from this wonderful, sweet man. Gavin picked Tiff up Monday night from her job; he looked at her and asked if she was ready to go home? Tiff said no, as they were riding toward the lake, Tiff was shouting in her boots, happy to know that Gavin had a few minutes to spare from his busy schedule to spend with her. After they parked, he looked at Tiff and said you got the house. So, from here on out what I do for you and with you is what I want to do. Tiff thought, "Oh God, I have on mix matched underwear". She start praying Oh God please do not let him move on me tonight, he will see I am not matching. Tiff and Gavin talked about everything except relationships, Gavin asked Tiff if she was ready to go? Tiff said ok. After standing, she just knew he would embrace her but he did not.

Gavin held Tiff's hand; she was so excited because he held her hand as they walked. As Gavin was taking Tiff home, she mentions to him that they were in a relationship because he held her hand as they walked. Gavin said to Tiff, no, as we were coming in I noticed you stumbled. I held your hand because I didn't want you to fall while you were with me. Tiff said to herself "she thought she had scored".

Tiff did not wash that hand for two days because Gavin had touched her. Two months after knowing Gavin, Gavin picked Tiff up after work; they went to the lake that was Tiff's and Gavin's favorite spot. Tiff made sure her underwear was matching just in case. They talked about business as usual. Gavin telling Tiff to stay focus and to make sure she screens everyone before hiring them. In addition, to make sure her paper work is always in on time. Tiff tried to read something between the lines.

Gavin found himself sitting too close to Tiff and quickly moved away, he almost fell off the bench, giving her more space. They sat that night for about two hours; he brought her home and kissed her on her lips. You could not tell Tiff this wasn't love. She brushed her teeth before going to bed; she pulled the kiss off her lips and laid it on the sink counter top until she finished brushing her teeth and then took both of her hands and placed the kiss back on her lips. As Tiff lay in bed, she wondered how she could get next to Gavin. What will it be like to be in his arms, in his bed, to taste him, and to feel his warmth? Gavin could never talk about his future because Tiff just knew she was included. Gavin mentioned he wanted to marry before the year was out. Tiff just knew he was talking about her. Tiff had her girlfriend Sandy helping her to pick out a wedding dress. Sandy asked Tiff did Gavin buy her a ring, she told Sandy, Gavin was just giving her a wedding ring instead of an engagement ring. Gavin did not have a clue this was going on. Sandy was trying to get Tiff friends together for a shower because Sandy began calling their friends together. Tiff said they were marrying before the year was over.

Gavin mentions that he and his daughter are taking a trip to Orlando and Tiff was ready to start packing. Gavin's daughter said, you can't go, Tiff's feelings were hurt. Tiff knew she had to work and she wanted to call in sick just to follow Gavin. Gavin, in talking, mentions to Tiff he was thinking about going to Louisiana for a few days.

Tiff went home, called her sister Virginia and told her that she and Gavin was getting married and they will spend time in Louisiana and that she was going to visit her while they were there.

Gavin called Tiff one night after ten o'clock. Tiff got so excited when she noticed the call was from him. She started pulling the sheets off the bed looking for her satin sheets, knowing Gavin was calling Tiff to let her know he was on his way. Tiff answered the phone with her most fine voice, asking Gavin what did she do to get this call. Tiff was batting her eyes and licking her lips, which Gavin didn't see. Gavin asked Tiff how she was doing. Her response was I am doing well since you called. Gavin asked Tiff what she was doing. Tiff said waiting on you. Tiff's body was getting all excited,

Gavin told Tiff he just called to remind her to write down everything she was going to need to get her business started and if there was anything he could do to help, she knew he was there for her. Gavin also told Tiff, she could and would do well if she stayed focus. Gavin told Tiff to have a good night and he hung the phone up. Tiff said to herself, she knew he wanted more, he just did not know how to ask.

Tiff was sitting home one night craving to hear from Gavin, so she called him. Gavin is a workaholic. Tiff called Gavin and asked him what he was doing. He told her working as always. Gavin asked Tiff what did she want, Tiff said I'll call back later, Gavin told her now that she had stopped him, go on and say what she wants. Tiff was so nervous because Gavin was always about business. Tiff said in her most sexy voice, I just want to know your favorite foods. Gavin told her he likes fish and chicken breast.

Tiff wondered if Gavin was a breast man because her chest was small and she wondered if she had to do implants, anything to get Gavin's attention. She asked about vegetables, he told her he does not do the green stuff, only sweet peas, green salad, and potato salad. Tiff smiled, she said yes, yes I can do him. She said to herself I could cook for him and put so much love into that food. Tiff asked Gavin about his favorite deserts hoping he would say Tiff but he said German chocolate cake and sweet potato pie.

Tiff said to herself "I am good to go because Publix and Wal-Mart sells good cakes and pies, she said thank God for Wall Mart". Tiff called Gavin the next night.

He asked may I help you, Tiff said to herself "Oh yes you can, but you won't," Gavin always answer the phone short. Tiff told Gavin she just called him to invite him to Thanksgiving dinner, Tiff was praying his daughter would spend Thanksgiving Day with her mother. Tiff knew if she got Gavin by himself at her house, she planned to get the most expensive wine that her budget could afford, get Gavin a little tipsy and then she knew he would make a move on her. He promised if nothing came up that he would be there.

Chapter 5
New House, New Start

Tiff just knew if she asked Gavin to move her into her new place she knew without a doubt that she would score. Gavin moved Tiff's queen size bed, as he was moving the bed Tiff was counting the seconds before he put the bed together. Gavin went to use the bathroom; Tiff had taken her clothes off just lying in the bed waiting on Gavin, with her blue matching panties. Gavin walks in the room and looks at Tiff and asked her where is the curtains for the bathroom, so I could hang them for you. Tiff asked Gavin why he could not do what she wanted him to do. Gavin looked at Tiff and said I am doing what you need me to do, and that is to hang the curtains.

Tiff asked Gavin to sit on the bed by her for a few minutes, he did. Tiff held Gavin's hand and asked him why he did not find her attractive? Gavin looked at Tiff and said I did not say that. Tiff told Gavin, men hit on her every day and she just cannot reach him. Gavin was a kind wealthy businessman. Gavin would do anything for Tiff.

It is so funny how Tiff is much older than Gavin but Tiff listens to Gavin.

Whatever Gavin tells her most of the time, he has thought it through.

Tiff lived in Tiff's world; Tiff thought she had all of the answers to everything. Nobody told Tiff what to do. Gavin tells Tiff something one time and he is through with it.

The old saying is before you get into a serious relationship you must first become friends. Tiff can truly say that about Gavin, he is her friend. Gavin brought a game over called the Corporate Ladder Board Game one night for them to play. Gavin was trying to play fair since Tiff did not know the game and he gave her a break. Once Tiff learned how to play, Tiff played ruthless. She did not give Gavin a break; Gavin looked at Tiff and said I will know the next time. The Corporate Ladder Board Game is a fun game.

There were days when Tiff wanted to hear from Gavin but he did not call. Tiff did not bother him; she just went on her daily chores hoping to hear from him.

Tiff did not work the Wednesday before Thanksgiving. Tiff went to the salon and brought a real pretty wig. She also got her hair fixed just in case the wig came off in the heat of passion, she would still be cute.

Tiff had her nails and toes done, she did not know whether Gavin was a toe man or not she just wanted everything in place. Tiff got to the salon at eight thirty that morning and left at five that evening.

Tiff went to the mall; she paid $200.00 for perfume she did not know how Gavin wanted his women to smell, loud, or mild or soft. Tiff looked at all kinds of sleepwear. She did not know if Gavin liked boxers or bikinis. She brought three different cuts; she knew Gavin would like at least one set, she did not know which, she just wanted to make sure. Tiff brought new satin sheets just for her Gavin.

Tiff tossed and turned all night waiting for the day to come so she can lay her eyes on her Gavin. Tiff got up at six o' clock Thanksgiving morning just to make sure everything was right when Gavin got there. Tiff brought a ham already sliced and cooked. She did not know whether she should bake it or what.
Tiff read the directions on the ham; the ham had several directions. Tiff called her friend Vanessa, to ask her which direction to use. Vanessa told Tiff to calm down and use the common sense one. Just put it in the oven fifteen minutes before Gavin arrives. Tiff asked Vanessa, suppose Gavin gets here fifteen minutes before two o' clock.

Vanessa told her to think about something to talk about for fifteen minutes. Tiff thanked Vanessa. Tiff wanted to cook macaroni and cheese from scratch. Tiff had seen her father boil water for the macaroni, but Tiff could not figure out if she should put everything in the pot at one time or not. It was seven thirty Tiff's time and four thirty a.m. Tiff sister's time. Tiff woke her sister up to ask her how to cook macaroni and cheese from scratch. Tiff's sister Linda asked Tiff whom was she cooking for so early in the morning. Tiff explained to Linda that Gavin was coming over for Thanksgiving. Linda asked Tiff what time Gavin was coming over, Tiff told her two o'clock. Linda asked Tiff what else are you cooking. Tiff told her she was cooking ham, macaroni and cheese, sweet peas, dinner rolls, and ice tea. Linda told her that she should start cooking at one thirty. Linda told Tiff it made no sense to get up this early.

Linda told Tiff she does not cook and gave her husband Emanuel the phone. He asked Tiff to get a pen and pad because he did not want her to forget and have to call back.
Tiff thanked him. Tiff said to herself, I am on top of my ham, my macaroni, now I got to deal with the peas. Tiff was trying to open a can of sweet peas and cut her finger on the can.

She bled so much she had to go to the emergency room. She sat in the emergency room from nine a.m. until twelve noon. Tiff asked the nurses how long is the wait because she had to get back home, realizing this was a holiday and they always take trauma first. She was walking the floor because she knew she had to be back by two o' clock. She was not letting anything stand in the way of her being with Gavin.

Tiff left the hospital all upset because she could not see the doctor. Tiff was fussing all the way home. After Tiff got home she wrapped her finger with toilet tissue and scotch tape, she had to finish her cooking because Gavin was coming.

Tiff called Walter from next door, asking him to please come over and open the can of peas for her. Tiff was so excited she told Walter about the wonderful man she had met. After Tiff poured the peas in the pot, she knew she had to put something in the peas, she knew she had to put salt and pepper but she didn't know what else she had to put in.
Tiff called her friend Earline in Tennessee to ask her what to put in her sweet peas other than salt and pepper. Tiff had to tell Earline all about how Gavin is so wonderful, sweet, and kind.

Earline told Tiff she had to put a little margarine, a little salt and pepper Earline knew if you told Tiff to much she would forget.

Tiff was so proud of her dinner; she said all she has to do is warm her rolls. Tiff looked at the clock and noticed it was one thirty. Tiff jumps in the shower, singing her favorite song I do not have to be lonely any more she thought. As soon as Tiff gets out the shower and drying her body thinking about Gavin the doorbell rang, it was Gavin and Kasha. Tiff said to herself, I just knew he was going to bring her, that little snot. Tiff said oh well since he brought her she might as well make the best of it. Tiff asked Kasha if she wanted to help her set the table, Kasha said nope, Tiff said to herself, you little snot. Gavin looked so damn good to Tiff, he smelled so good, and you had to be close to him to smell his cologne. Tiff said to herself, oh if I could get a little closer but she knew it would not happen for Thanksgiving because he had that little snot with him. Gavin had on navy blue slacks black shoes, blue and yellow button down shirt, navy socks, with his dreamy sexy bed room eyes. Every time Tiff saw Gavin it was like Christmas, he was so cool, handled himself like this was his world and he was just renting us a space.

Gavin noticed Tiff's finger and arm was wrapped poorly. Gavin asked Tiff to come here, he asked Tiff what happened. Tiff was acting as if her finger was about to drop off while Gavin ministered to her. Gavin goes to his Z and finds a roll of tape and rewrapped Tiff's finger. Tiff forgot all about the meal until Kasha said she was hungry. Tiff goes in the kitchen; she noticed she forgot to put the ham in the oven. She checked the macaroni and noticed she forgot to turn the oven on. Tiff was trying to be so careful not to let anything touch where Gavin had touched.

Tiff sitting down while nursing her hand that Gavin had touched, Kasha asked when are we going to eat. Tiff was in a daze behind Gavin's touch. She just sat the food on the table and she did not want anything to touch where Gavin had touched her. Tiff's bread was over cooked; it was hard. Her macaroni was still running, she sprinkled too much salt in the peas. Kasha looked at the food and said daddy, what is this; I just can't eat this.
Kasha said daddy lets go buy some chicken. Gavin being the gentleman he is and the father that he is, he was trying to tell Tiff he would take a ring check so her feelings would not be hurt. Tiff was so hurt, she put it all on Gavin's daughter the reason her day was spoiled.

Tiff was so tired she fell asleep knowing there was no way for her to get Gavin. Tiff's sisters from California called Tiff asking her about her date. Tiff broke down and starts to cry, telling Linda that Gavin's daughter messed up her food. Linda being a counselor, always has to get to the bottom of everything. She told Tiff the little girl didn't mess up her food, she was just over anxious. Tiff told Linda she's always taking up for other people.

Two days later, Tiff called Gavin to ask him would he drop in and look at her computer. Tiff told Gavin her computer has frozen and Gavin told Tiff he would be there in a couple of hours. Gavin did look at Tiff's computer and he saw nothing wrong with the computer. Tiff stared at Gavin all hungry eyed; Gavin asked Tiff what was wrong? Tiff asked Gavin in her most sexy voice to kiss her, Tiff had brushed and flossed all morning. Gavin looked at Tiff, smiled and said I will see you later. Tiff thought to herself "he could not be gay, he walks like a man, and he talks like a man". He has no female traits. Tiff began to wonder what was wrong with her. She's the same chocolate brown that other men chased. Her figure was still the same, her butt was still pretty cool, and she has a professional job. What was his problem?

Did he think he was too good for her?
Nobody knew Tiff could sing but Tiff. Maybe Gavin did not care for her singing and knew if they were in a relationship, he would have to deal with that on a daily basis. Tiff had never seen a man like Gavin; he showed no interest in her. Tiff wondered if Gavin had bad eyesight or did some other pretty woman like Tiff abuse him. Tiff was sexy from head to toe. Tiff never left home without some man wanting to be with her, but not Gavin.

Tiff brought a German chocolate cake from Wal-Mart. She took it home and put it on one of her cake plates; gave it to Gavin and told him she baked it from scratch just for him. Gavin took the cake and told her thanks. He knew it was store brought; Gavin took the cake to the homeless shelter as a small donation from him. Gavin did not care for sweets that much and the old saying is the way to a man's heart is through his stomach. Gavin was not ready to give his heart to anyone, especially Tiff. A week passed, Tiff heard nothing from Gavin, she passed Gavin's house the only person she saw was little Kasha outside playing. Tiff thought maybe if she became friends with Gavin's little brat, just maybe the brat could help her with her father.

Gavin picked Tiff up one night and took her on the lake under the gazebo. They sat and talked for a couple hours, he even held her hand. She did everything in her power to maintain her composure. Tiff is wondering where has this man been all of her life. Gavin did not talk that much but when he spoke, he had something to say. He was a smooth thinker and talker. All of Gavin's conversations were always about business on how to make a dollar or how to save a dollar. Tiff wore her best matching bra and bikinis every time she and Gavin went anywhere just in case, thinking he would ask her but he never did. Gavin never tried to kiss her; he's always that perfect gentleman.

One night, Tiff asked Gavin why he never tried to kiss her. Gavin told Tiff he does not want a relationship based on sex nor on lust. He wants to build a solid relationship on love, trust, and friendship. Tiff said to herself "who needs all of that". After that, Tiff looked at Gavin in a different way; she said "I got to have him". I must have him because he is a real, real, real man and he is a brother. Gavin told Tiff how he brought a pair of ten-dollar tennis shoes while driving a big body Mercedes Benz. Would you call him tight or would you say he just purchase the things he like?

One dollar or one hundred dollars all depends on what a person likes. Gavin took Tiff to Wendy's one night, she does not know if the burger was good because she was with Gavin but the burger was delicious. It really was not about the food it was about being in his presence.

Gavin drove a 300ZX, it did not matter where Gavin went as long as she was with him, with the top down and she wore her big hat.

Gavin brought Tiff home one day, Tiff looked at Gavin and said to him, she knows that he is a blessing from God. Gavin tells Tiff, God let them cross each other's path to help her with her business. Tiff told Gavin it was more than that because that is what her body dictates to her. Tiff explained to Gavin, no one makes her body crave the way Gavin do. Tiff also told Gavin that he would never find a love like hers, someone who loves him tenderly.
Tiff called Kasha, Gavin's daughter, and asked her what did Gavin enjoy doing? Kasha told Tiff her father enjoyed playing with her and he enjoyed spending time with her. Kasha told Tiff her dad does like her. Tiff hung up the phone and said damn that is a smart little girl; I am going to buy her something special.

Chapter 6
California Get-A-Way

Tiff tells Gavin she has to get away; Tiff decides to go to San Francisco, CA. to spend time with her sister to try to get Gavin out of her system.

Tiff asked Gavin to bring her to the airport, he agrees to; she also gave Gavin a key to her house. She asked him to watch her house while she was away. Tiff asked Gavin would he miss her after she leave. Gavin says to Tiff, sure I will miss you. Tiff, you are my friend and business partner. Tiff looks at Gavin and mumble yea, yea.

Tiff flight leaves at seven a.m.; Gavin was at Tiff's place at five thirty a.m. He's looking so good early in the morning. He wore black jeans and a red pull over. Gavin knocked on Tiff's door. Tiff made her way to Gavin's arms, he held her as if she was a sister in Christ, with her husband looking. As Gavin was taking Tiff to the airport, Tiff made Gavin promise that he would miss her. Tiff gets on the plane and she is sitting next to Aaron Bing, the Jazz player. Aaron, his producer and his manager was on their way to appear on the "Wendy Williams Show" from there to the Late Show with "David Letterman".

He and Tiff had a good conversation. He autographs a poster for Tiff and gives her his latest CD and his phone number. Tiff was excited, she was happy that she had a real reason to call Gavin.

Tiff had an hour layover in North Carolina. She called Gavin and they talked for a while. Tiff asked Gavin had he start missing her yet, he told her she just left. She had not given him time to miss her.

The ride from North Carolina to California was five hours. Tiff slept four of the five hours. She was so tired of thinking about Gavin; she needed the sleep. Tiff called her sister in Louisiana to let her know she had to get away for a while because she was making herself ill trying to figure this man out. Tiff's sister said, she has given up on trying to figure men out.

Tiff tells her sister she has given up too, but this man just dropped out of Heaven just for her. Tiff told her sister her name is written all over this man. Tiff's sister made her feel a little sad reminding her of her failed relationships. After Tiff hung up, Tiff starts talking to God. Tiff reminded God that he said if she be happy in him, he would give her the desires of her heart.

Tiff said Lord you said you would withhold no good thing from me and Gavin is a good thing. You said I am to be submissive. I do not have Gavin to be submissive to. You said women are to take care of their husbands, how can I if I do not have Gavin.

Tiff called her sister in San Francisco and told her she was on her way but she was not good company because Gavin is not getting the picture. Her sister Linda tells Tiff to come on, she knows she can help her to get over the man that she never had. It was a good flight; it was sixty-five degrees when Tiff left Florida and thirty-five degrees when Tiff got to North Carolina.

Tiff had not traveled in a while, she forgot they no longer serve free food on the plane, only water and drinks everything else you had to buy. Tiff was waiting on the food tray to come around, nothing, not even a cracker. Tiff wondered if nine eleven did that or was the economy still bad. Tiff thought about Sanford and Son, how Fred traveled with fried greasy chicken wings. Tiff was thinking she just might do the same thing going back because the food on the plane was a little too high for her. Tiff's plane landed in San Francisco, CA. at twelve thirty p.m. The weather was fifty degrees.

In one day, Tiff experienced three different weather climates. The airport in San Francisco, CA. was so busy. Tiff lives in a big city but it is a big country city. After Tiff got with her sisters, it was boring as ever. Tiff baby sister was giving her husband a birthday party, all of Emanuel's family was there. They cooked so much food for just one day. The mountains in San Francisco were so pretty, it is a good place to visit but not for Tiff to live. The leaves on the trees were just beautiful. Tiff thought, it is amazing how God spoke this great big world into existence.

Emanuel's family enjoys cooking, Tiff told Emanuel's family about this wonderful man she met. Tiff explained to them this was her last time around in life and she have to be able to cook for this man. Emanuel's family put Tiff on the potatoes, showing Tiff how to hold the knife so she would not cut too much potato off with the peeling. One of Emanuel's sisters went to Dollar Tree and brought Tiff a potato peeler so Tiff could get it right. Tiff saying in her mind, all you got to do is buy potato salad from the store but just in case Gavin was picky, she will know how to make potato salad from scratch. Emanuel's family felt that since Gavin was from Louisiana, he would enjoy eating the kind of food that he was custom to eating.

Tiff told them he loves sweet potato pie; they taught Tiff the best way to make sweet potato pie from scratch was to bake the sweet potatoes first, so the sweet flavor would remain in the potatoes.

Tiff being Tiff had to call back home to check on her friends. Tiff had a friend back home she knew was dying but just didn't want to accept Christ. Tiff called her Saturday morning, trying to get her to accept Christ but she just will not. Tiff even gave her a little sermon, telling her it's not God's will for her to perish and we were not invited to go to hell, that hell was for the devil and his angles, our invitation was Heaven. Tiff goes on to tell her who will take care of her baby when she passed away: it really bothered Tiff.

When people refuse to accept God, when he has done so much for us, when all she had to do is say, Lord I repent of my sin, save me, and believe in him. In addition, God will do the rest. She just will not do it.

Even if it is not Heaven, we can appreciate him for this life. Tiff has learned the secret on how to move God and how to touch God. She told her friend when she was younger, how she had cancer.

The doctor told Tiff the same thing he told her friend, he could not do anything else for her. Tiff being a preacher's daughter, she learned how to pray, how to turn her plate down, how to get in the word and how to pray herself to sleep. Tiff made God a promise, she got real serious, she told God if he would heal her, she would tell everybody she see about God and that is what she does, she always find a way to ease it in to her conversation.

Tiff's oldest sister invited Tiff to a "Woman of War" annual tea brunch. "Share your favorite tea cup"; that was out in Stockton, CA. That gave Tiff and Jeanette time to bond again. Jeanette has a lovely home; she has a granny apple tree in her backyard and beautiful flowers in her front yard. Jeanette lives in an old neighborhood, the houses are beautiful. The food was very good. Tiff asked one of the sisters that was serving the food if they had to get up very early to prepare the food. The sister looked at her and smiled, she said, yes we did, and the little sister told Tiff she hopes she enjoyed the food.

Tiff was thinking spiritual; she was thinking like David when he said, my cup is full and running over since the Lord saved me. However, they talked about their own personal teacup.

Tiff thought about it and remembered she never had a teacup that meant that much to her. The only cup that meant that much to her was a Styrofoam cup, the kind you use and then you threw it away. Those girls did their thing. It was interesting everywhere Tiff went, it reminded her of Gavin in some way. The lady was talking about how we as women chase men and the scripture says, "whosoever findeth a wife findeth a good thing". Tiff thought, sometimes we have to help God because he is so busy at times, especially when it came to Gavin. The speaker talked about hurting women, women who had been abused, raped and women who had been dumped for one reason or another. Tiff thought about it and said thank God she has never been raped or abused but her main thing was the times she was dumped. She thought maybe being dumped was a form of abuse. Tiff thought to herself sometimes women are the abusers.

Sometimes, Tiff talks to men and they tell her how their woman or wife abused them or how they were dumped also. Tiff knows the things that make the world go around is pain, suffering, joy, peace, and love. Tiff thought, oh, if she could just get Gavin to love her. After Tiff and her oldest sister left the tea, and went to strip mall just to look.

Neither tiff nor her sister had shopping money. Tiff's sister has a closet full of shoes and clothes. Tiff's sister said she has given up on brothers; she is going white or African. Tiff told Jeanette she just couldn't do white, Tiff told Jeanette white folks are good to work with, to go to church with, have conversation with but not to bed with. Tiff told Jeanette when you see all of the high yellow folks out here that mean Old Master had an affair with someone great grandmother or grandmother, who could not and did not have the strength to say no.

Tiff thought about the time her uncle was hung from a tree for just looking at a white woman and she will never ever let one touch her in that way. Her sister Jeanette told Tiff, she has to let it go. The world is changing and we have to move on. Tiff told Jeanette she has moved on and that there are still sweet, kind, educated, God fearing black men who still respect their women. There are still black men who are still willing to do the right thing when it comes to their women. There are still black men who want to be home and raise their own children or men who will not be put through that baby mama drama. Tiff's sister looks at her and asked, what planet was she on.

Being Submissive

Tiff thought about it, black women just do not get it. Just think about it, God made everything, he spoke everything in to existence, but when he got ready to make man, the Father, Son, and Holy Spirit came together. God said let us make man in our image our likeness. This same God said he wanted praise from everybody and everything that is breathing, he want praises from it or them.

Men are made in God's image; they want their women to praise them, that's why we are missing it. No, we as women get so biggity and say that is what he is supposed to do, why should I praise him for taking out the garbage? It is his garbage just as much as it is mine. Why should I praise him for taking care of his own children? All men have to be praised. Tiff thought about it, what is wrong with a woman looking up at her man and saying thank you for choosing me. Tiff thought about it and said that is the key to a good relationship, we have to know how to praise a brother. Tiff thought that is the reasons she have had so many struggles in relationships, it was not the large things, it was the small things.

Tiff just did not listen, did not know how to listen to reason, it had to be Tiff's way.

Tiff is not saying all men are there but Tiff feels that with the proper respect, which is so hard when the brother is stupid but that is what we picked. Just maybe if we worked with whatever we saw when we got with them, just maybe it would have worked. Now that God has done a real job in Tiff, she hates to admit it, but most relationships Tiff had, could have worked. The reason she say this, she feels that if she would have not been thinking about Tiff, what Tiff was not getting out of the relationship, being humble which is hard, being submissive, which is even harder. We quote the scripture "I can do all things through Christ that strengthens me" and we cannot hold a relationship together.

Tiff thought about how much power we as black women have but we use a lot of it for destruction. That is why Tiff knows that she could be the best thing for and to Gavin because she has learned her lesson the hard way.

All she need is for God to give her just one more chance at love. Tiff said she would run Gavin's bath water; then she thought, most men take showers, why can't he run his own bath water.

Tiffs said she would take the time and bathe him, dry him off and lotion that fine body any time he lets her. Tiff thought she would spoon-feed Gavin, why, because he would be her prized possession. Tiff knows giving men that much attention; they would do anything for her because they would love the attention. Think about it ladies, all or none.

If we find another man, the relationship will start out good; what happens? He stayed out a little too long, we start fussing, not trusting. If our man has a bad day, he may come home and take it out on his strength, which is us, and if we are tuned into him, we can see his mood swing is different. That is when we think about the song "when something is wrong with my baby something is wrong with me". Tiff feels if babies are not involved, we should drop everything and try to find out what is going on and give him our undivided attention. Tiff feels that if a woman is working along with her man and if by any means, the husband is laid off, and cannot find a job but is giving his best looking for a job. After six-months has passed and he feels beat down, his self worth starts to slowly fade and he wakes up one morning saying I'm not going out today, I'm going to just stay home in bed because I'm just tired; I've looked and looked but I just haven't found anything.

We add insult to injury; we start calling them lazy bums and tell them we are not going to take care of them. They already feel bad; we go on and on. Before we know it, he is drinking, smoking dope, trying to sell dope or find another woman who sees so much more in him than we did.

They get together and go farther than they went with us. Now we are mad, when all we had to do was work with the brother and be a little more patient.

Tiff said she would never make any more of those foolish mistakes with Gavin, why, because as Al Green says "She is so tired of being alone". Tiff is so tired of failing in relationships.

Gavin is that man that Tiff can be so proud of until the day she dies. She promised herself she will listen to him and she will not talk down to him, she will give him his due respect.

Tiff said she has never really worked on a relationship but she promised herself and God if she got Gavin she will take time and work on that relationship.

The Party

Later that same Saturday night, Tiff's baby sister, Linda, who has been married for thirty years to her husband, Emanuel, gave a surprise birthday party for him, it was real nice. All of his brothers and sisters came from Louisiana, except one. Emanuel had no clue of the party. Emanuel was surprised she invited two hundred people; the place was full. Linda invited a local Christian comedian. She talked about growing up in a family with fourteen children, they lived in a three-bed room house, she was good. Tiff's sister also invited J-RED from Oakland, he was very good. He talked about being a holiness preacher's kid growing up back in the day, he talked about how PK kids (preacher kids) did Halloween different from CK kids (Christian kids) he was real funny. Emanuel received many gifts.

Tiff really enjoyed spending time with her oldest sister, Jeanette, she lives in Stockton, Ca. Jeanette works for the State Congressman, everybody knows her. When she is invited to a function, people respond to her as if she was a top dog. For the last ten years, she has been working heavily in politics. After the function, Tiff and Jeanette went to Linda's for a little while.

Tiff was ready to shut it down. It was eleven thirty Tiff's time and two a.m. Gavin's time. Tiff knew it was too late to call anybody just to ask if he missed her.

Sunday Morning

Tiff got up Sunday morning, called Gavin to see what was going on in his world. Tiff knew how the world goes, when one woman is interested there are other women coming out of the woodwork. That is why Tiff had to check in every day so Gavin would know that she was still interested.

Tiff and Jeanette meets Linda and other family members at church. Church had already started when they got there. Tiff had a hairline run in her stockings; going to this church for the first time, Tiff could not afford to let the church people see runs in her stockings. Tiff had Jeanette going out the way looking for a Wal-Mart so she could buy a pair of stockings. Jeannette told Tiff she was so unorganized, she should have brought more than one pair of stockings. Tiff told her she did; the ones she wore Saturday had a little mud on the toe from the bad weather, they were black, the ones she was wearing Sunday was chocolate brown. Tiff wondered why her sister would want her to wear black stockings with a brown suit. Tiff gets to church on Sunday and ninety five percent of the people were the same people Tiff saw the night before, Tiff was looking for new faces.

Linda waited outside the church for Tiff and Jeanette. Linda was fussing at Tiff, telling her she is always late for everything. Linda's husband is a preacher.

Linda invited all four of Emanuel's sisters and his brothers to Church. They were on time except Tiff and Jeanette. Tiff wanted to sit in the back but because Linda was active in church, she marched Tiff all the way to the second row; if Tiff had known that, she would have worn a shorter skirt. There was a nice looking man playing the key board, Tiff asked Linda who was that man. Linda told Tiff that he is the Pastor and do not put your hungry looking eyes on him. Tiff automatically knew his wife or woman because she was sitting on the front pew, smiling, saying Amen louder than anybody, standing up, and smiling from ear to ear. Tiff looked at her bulletin and knew she had to be the first lady. She kept looking at Tiff smiling as to say you are going to be my friend not his. I am letting you know I am the first lady and it is going to stay that way.

The good Rev. was a good teacher, he was not a whooper and a hollerer, and he talked on giving: "If you keep your hands closed, you will never receive anything", he came from the book of Acts.

His subject was, "I care".
Tiff wanted to see how much he cared but the first lady would not bring him over. After church, Tiff told the first lady her family was cooking and asked the first lady to bring the good Rev. over. Tiff put on her tight fitting jeans but the first lady and the good Rev. never made it.

The Family

Linda has three children: Elizabeth, Germaine, and John. Linda raised her children on black and white television with no cable. Elizabeth is a lawyer; Germaine has his own private practice. John, twelfth grade making straight A's, his goal is the NBA. Elizabeth married a sports commentator; they have two beautiful children, Zion and Mason. Zion talks like a little cartoon character, Mason, her little son, looks like a Troll, he has more hair than he has body. The kids are so cute. They are all over the place. Germaine and his wife live in Sunny Valley, CA. They have a two-week-old baby girl; she is spoiled because she has two sets of grandparents and a great grandmother. Germaine closed his practice down for six weeks to help his wife with the baby. His wife Pat is a youth therapist. Tiff brought a game for the family to play called the Corporate Ladder but she just could not get them all stable enough to play. Emanuel's sister, Pearl, flew in from Louisiana, with her grandson Malcolm. Malcolm is too smart for his own good. Emanuel has three more sisters: Mae is a very sweet woman, she does what she can for anybody, she has so much patience's with Tiff, and in fact, all of Emanuel sisters do.

Ann, she is something like Tiff. She knows she is what the men need. When Ann finds a man with a good job, she just sits down and let him pay all of her bills because she just got it like that. Ann tells her men, you have to pay to boss this. Ann makes sure her men are well satisfied because when she shows the bills she expects to be satisfied. Ann has two sons; she is teaching them very good: if you get a woman, you have to take care of her. The women are standing in line to get to Ann's boys.

Marie is the baby girl, she's tall and fair. Marie married a Puerto Rican, he cannot speak a drop of English but when Marie put it on Rico he understand the English real well. Marie is her own woman; she goes and comes when she feels like it. When she goes out with her friends, Rico tries to get angry. Marie tells him I told you I was going out with my friends, she does tell him, he just do not understand the language.

Emanuel's younger brother came to the party also. He thinks he is so cool that every time he visits California he has to meet a new woman. While visiting California, Pop and Marie, went out on the town. Pop left his cell phone, around three a.m. Pop's Louisiana woman called, Tiff answered the phone, happy to tell the Louisiana woman that he has gone out with his woman in California.

The house was full, Tiff had been staying with her oldest sister in Stockton, CA. Tiff youngest sister insisted on her spending the night in Tracy, CA. Tiff did, and left her cell phone card in Stockton, CA. which is thirty miles from Tracy and nobody would take her to get her cord. Tiff was having all kinds of fits because she needed to be in contact with Gavin and could not.

Tiff tried every cell phone cord in Linda's house until she found one that fitted. Tiff struck gold when she found one. Tiff let it charge five minutes and called Gavin. Gavin answered on the third ring. Tiff was so happy; she asked Gavin did he miss her? Gavin being so sweet said yes, Tiff could not stop smiling. Tiff got quiet, Gavin asked Tiff what was wrong, she told Gavin he had just said the magic words 'he missed her'. Tiff asked Gavin what he was doing. Gavin told her he was washing dishes. Tiff thought if she was with Gavin she could put gloves on and wash dishes for Gavin. Tiff just could not see a man like Gavin washing dishes, not Gavin. Tiff thought, the hands Gavin is washing dishes with, he could be stroking her, the time he put into washing dishes he could be spending with her.

Tiff and her sisters had dinner together. After dinner, they went back to Jeanette's office for their own business meeting. Tiff and her family planned a cruise in June. In addition, they were talking about having a foundation for their mother. Tiff caught a bad cold in the weather with her sisters, she was so upset knowing she would be going home in a couple of days and just in case Gavin wanted a kiss, she would have to tell him no because of her cold.

Tiff's youngest sister is a therapist; Tiff went to work with her. She has her own office; Tiff thought she should be laying on the sofa. After Linda finished her client, she and Tiff headed out to Stockton to a Successful Thinking meeting, "I am successful". The speaker said if your circle of friends is not on the same page that you are on, just let them go. The food was interesting; they asked all first time visitors to make a small video explaining their company. Tiff was so excited even though she felt like crap. Tiff called Gavin and asked him if it was ok to do the video advertising his games. Gavin thanked Tiff, if she was not over excited she probably would have done a better job but just hearing Gavin's voice messed Tiff up bad. After Tiff left, she went straight home and called Gavin.

Tiff enjoyed spending time with her sisters in California but they just were not Gavin. Tiff never talked about Gavin and that made her sisters inquire more and more about him.

Her sister Jeanette asked Tiff what is so important about this man. Tiff told her that Gavin listens when she talks and he hears her. She said ok and what else, Tiff also said he see her as a professional person with her head on straight and he makes her feel like the sky is her limit. Tiff told her sister, it is the little things that Gavin does. She told her sister Gavin is a nice looking man with a brain, with his head on straight, he's business minded. He is not always pulling on Tiff but sometimes she wished he would.

Gavin designed this Corporate Ladder Board Game: Is it a game or is it reality. Tiff, her sisters Linda and Jeannette and Jeannette's friend played the game. They played so ruthless. Tiff was trying to tell them how the game goes and they did not hear her. Tiff called Gavin and she gave the phone to her sister. Gavin explained the game to them again. Tiff sister who just made herself President refused to let go of that position.

Tiff's youngest sister suggested that they start over and play the game right. However, Jeanette would not give up the position. Jeanette was like Tiff as long as the money was coming in, she was good but when she had to pay bills, it took her all night to pay one person.

The game was meant for fun but they took it to a completely new level. Jeanette wanted to know with her lawyer, could she just file bankrupt, shut the company down, and just sit on her money. At the end of the game, Tiff had more money than anyone did. Linda tells Tiff you have to have liquid assets. A multi-millionaire does not just walk up to a place with a hand full of money and say I want to buy this hotel. He had liquid assets.

Tiff told them it is ok if they will not sell her stuff in America for cash, she will buy an Island in a third world country for her and her money. Lu, Jeannette's friend, asked Tiff would she let her come live on her Island with her Tiff told her nope because she might have to take some of her money to buy Lu some food. Tiff let them know she was not giving up anything. Tiff never saw a game played so ruthless. Linda asked her 17-year-old son would he buy her a mansion. He told her nope, tell her husband to buy her a house, he said, mama this is a dog eat dog world.

It was so funny when the game was over, the question was asked, would they really act like that if they had real money. Everybody but Tiff said they would not. Tiff said she would act the same not giving up anything.

The "Corporate Ladder Game" allow players to experience corporate life, rich with realistic elements. Decision-making, risk taking and aggressive behavior are the cornerstones of the game. Based on the principal of climbing the "Corporate Ladder", it is a fast-paced race from getting a job to becoming President. Strategy, managing money, making sound decisions and learning from your mistakes are just a few of the practices you learn by playing. They must be careful because competitors are working at the same time to beat them to the top! In this world, players must think on their feet, wheeling and dealing up the "Corporate Ladder". Confidence is gained by playing well and taking risks. The wealthiest player wins.

As Tiff lay in bed thinking about Gavin, she remembered he told her the way for her to pay him back for the service he rendered to her, once she starts making money, if she saw someone who needed a little help, for Tiff to invest in their project.

Tiff is older than Gavin but she will get out of the box in every way. Gavin tells Tiff it is ok to think out of the box but do not get too far out of the box. Tiff told her sisters, Gavin has three businesses and two or three different kind of business cards. They asked Tiff if she had business cards? She told them no, because she do not have a business. They told Tiff everybody has business cards. Tiff finds another reason to call Gavin and ask him if she can attach his web page to her business cards. Gavin being Gavin said yes.
Jeanette gets online and finds the perfect card. She changed Tiff's email address and designed the business cards. Linda, Tiff's youngest sister paid for them. Tiff thanked them. Her sisters told her they have never seen her act this way and whatever they can do to help they will do it. It was amazing how Tiff and her two sisters got back together after ten or twelve years of bickering over the little stuff.

Chapter 7
Back to Tiff World

When Tiff got off the plane and went to claim her luggage, she saw Gavin. Tiff felt so good to see the man who she admires the most waiting for her, wearing that sexy smile with those beautiful bedroom eyes.

Gavin asked Tiff how was the flight. It was a good flight, she said. Tiff wondered and wondered why Gavin was not locked down in a relationship.

Was it because he had a daughter and thought she would be mistreated or he wanted to wait until she finished school before he made a commitment to another woman.

Did he think a woman wanted his money by him being so kind, he would not have to tell her no when she asked for shopping money.

Did he think because he was so sweet that somebody like Tiff would be stupid, jealous and that would interfere with his businesses, the kind of work he does, maybe the jealousy would ruin his businesses. Maybe he enjoys sleeping by himself.

Tiff thought they could get twin beds or a king size bed. Tiff wondered if she and Gavin shared a king size bed would Tiff get any sleep or would she just lay there and watch Gavin sleep.

Tiff kept wondering why Gavin was not in love with a woman, she wondered has Gavin had a sex change and did not know how to tell Tiff. Tiff was so in love with Gavin, even if he had a sex change, Tiff would not have cared. Tiff thought if Gavin had a sex change, he carried himself so masculine.

Gavin never cursed, he always treated Tiff with the highest of respect. Gavin was concerned about Tiff's well being. After Tiff moved in her new place, she thought she heard someone breaking in on her, it could have been her imagination, but Tiff called Gavin. Gavin told Tiff to call 911 but Tiff told Gavin she was too nervous to call 911. Gavin went to see about Tiff. Tiff thought Gavin would hold her and tell her he was there for her, instead, he left his SUV and called someone to come pick him up. He wanted whoever tried or whomever Tiff thought she heard to think he was there and as long as they knew a man was on the property, they would not bother Tiff any more.

Tiff thought that the SUV could not do for her what Gavin could have done. When Gavin left, Tiff said to herself, he is so precious, he told Tiff to give the police a call if she heard anything else and for Tiff to call him if she needed anything else.

Gavin is such a gentleman. Gavin called Tiff the next morning. Tiff did not know he was in her yard when he called her. He asked Tiff what she was doing, Tiff told Gavin she was stepping out of the tub. Gavin told Tiff he was standing in her yard. She grabbed her trench coat, nothing else, she ran outside to greet Gavin, legs ashy, she did not think about that, all she thought about was seeing Gavin. Gavin noticed someone had been in Tiff's yard, he knew she was telling the truth.

Gavin kissed Tiff on the lips telling her he will be back to fix the damage on her house. Tiff thought when she least expected it, that is when Gavin kisses her. Tiff went to church. Church was good and long; something just told Tiff it was time to go. Gavin and Kasha was at Tiff's house playing maintenance man. Tiff was so happy the Bible said, "God calls those things that are not as though they were". When Tiff saw Gavin and Kasha, Tiff said look at my family. Gavin connected her washing machine; he fixed the light in her utility room, and her front light. Tiff said to herself this man is so sweet, so caring, so precious, he understands everything but the fact that he belongs to Tiff. This man hung Tiff's curtains and put her bed up, he moved her, and he hooked up her stove. The only thing he asked for was a glass of tea.

Gavin sits on Tiff's sofa with his arm stretched out on the back of it. Tiff always wanted to sit in Gavin arms but she felt if she did, he might just get up and leave.

Tiff was asked one Sunday to give her testimony in church. Tiff had to tell how her life had been going downhill; she could not find a job anywhere. She told the congregation how she lived on nine hundred dollars last year and how God had blessed her. Tiff lights were never turned off and she was never homeless.

After Tiff could not find a job, she decided to go to nursing school. Tiff told the Dean she could pay one hundred and twenty dollars a month. Tiff also told the congregation how she had to sell her best clothes to buy bus passes to get to school every day. Tiff had her best boots for sale, a girl wanted Tiff's boots but did not have any money, and Tiff exchanged a hairdo for her boots. Tiff also told them how she prayed and prayed for God to tell her where to go for a part time job because she really needed a job. As Tiff prayed and prayed, the Lord dropped in her spirit where to go.

Tiff walks up to the front desk, she asked Mrs. Johnson, the lady sitting behind the desk, if they were hiring or did she know anybody that was hiring. Mrs. Johnson answered yes, we are. Tiff said "Thank you sweet Jesus". Mrs. Johnson printed an application. Tiff asked if she could take the application home and Mrs. Johnson said yes. Tiff wanted to bring the application home so she could pray over it. Tiff remembered the scripture "In all thy ways acknowledge him, and he will direct your path". Tiff had her own prayer meeting over her application. Tiff took the application back to Mrs. Johnson. Mrs. Johnson told Tiff they would be interviewing in two weeks; she told Tiff they would give her a call. The job called her in two weeks for an interview and a simple test.

Tiff got through the interview and she passed the test with a high score. Tiff still had to do her drug screening and fingerprints. Tiff knew she had the job because she never used drugs. After she was hired, she prayed all night thanking God for the job.

Tiff went to school four days a week from nine until two. She worked from four to eight on Mondays and all day Friday and Saturday. Tiff had a little money to pay on a little something. Tiff called her property owner and told him she was working and that she was going to move in with a friend. The property owner asked Tiff why did she want to leave her little house, Tiff told him that she wanted to be able to pay him a little money. He advised Tiff to stay in her little house because women do fall out and he did not care to see her on the streets.

Tiff had to tell the congregation how God had blessed her with this wonderful man in her life; she had to tell the whole story. How she met Gavin, how he turned her thinking around, and how she thought she knew men. Tiff was like the woman at the well, I have met a man, a black man, a God fearing man, a man who strives to do the right thing by people, he lives by Bible Principles, he also raised his son by Bible Principles. He is like my mother, she always says it is just right to do right.

Tiff wondered when Gavin's parents raised him, did they realized how great of a job they had done. A man like Gavin could be a lover, he has all the attributes, he could have babies all over the place, but instead he only has two children of his own. We have to give a brother his due props. He could have been a sperm donor because he is so smart and kind. He could have been a pastor because he has the heart of a Pastor. This man has never done drugs, smoked, or drink. A man like Gavin can be very valuable to the community. I don't know the programs in the community that he's involved with but a man like Gavin you don't question, you just listen to him quietly and if you listen, you can and will learn his ways and the things that he does.

Tiff asked Gavin one day what makes him happy, he said and I quote him "The people that I help, striving to do their best, doesn't quit when they don't get it right the first few times."

Tiff asked Gavin what makes him sad, and I quote him "To see people, especially blacks, let life pass them by without putting forth an effort to try to do better, in other words, those who are on the planet Earth just for the ride".

Gavin feels that if a person put forth an effort, God will put someone in place to help and guide them alone the way. Gavin feels that people are without excuses.

You want it or you do not want it. He is a smart brilliant man, if a person is trying to accomplish something and fall short he will help you but he will not do it for you. That is what Tiff learned from him by being his friend.

If you invite Gavin to a gathering, if it is not about business he will not sit around and just shoot the bull. A little advice: if you have a barbeque, don't sit around dropping it like it's hot and drinking beer because he will get a plate and move on. This man was brought up in church, he knows the Lord, he has so much integrity, and he has ethics. Many brothers feel that it is ok to break the law but not Gavin. He believes in obeying the laws of the land.

The thing that is so interesting about this man, right now he is not in church but he does not bash the church. If you ask him why he does not go to church, he just says I do not. Tiff knows the Bible says, "Whosoever findeth a wife findeth a good thing and obtains favor from the LORD". Tiff knows that. Tiff's mothers' philosophy is do not be so excited about a churchman, if we as women, get a man that loves us, put God first, and everybody and everything behind us, that is the kind of man we want.

Because if he loves us, they will do anything for us, if we love God and live the life before them, they will be the one to say come on baby lets go to church.

Tiff had husbands and all kinds of men but she never found a man like Gavin. It is as if he is not real, they go out to eat, Gavin always bless the food. Tiffs' so called friends says that Gavin might hurt her. Tiff says big deal; Tiff says it is best to have met a man like Gavin and lost him than to have never found this wonderful man. Tiff feels like if a man like Gavin can be this nice to her and they are just friends, she can imagine what it would be like if they were in a relationship.

Tiff asked Gavin when she starts her business would he speak to her clients on Sundays, so she will not have to take them to church; he asked her why she could not do it. Tiff told Gavin it was a man thing. Gavin told Tiff he would do it. Tiff is looking forward to opening her business because she know once she is open, she knows within her heart of hearts he will be there making sure she is doing the right thing for herself. Tiff woke up one morning and poured her heart out to God. Tiff told God he has answered all of her prayers in everything she asked him for when she prayed.

Tiff asked God to please help her get over this man. Tiff stopped looking at Gavin through her natural eyes and started looking at Gavin through her spiritual eyes and what she had to bring to the table. She realized she is the King's kid and her father told her to ask anything in his name and he will provide for her.

Tiff had what it took to do anything that she put her heart to. It hit Tiff, it really hit Tiff, she finally realized what God was doing to and through her. Tiff had to learn how to be humble. Tiff had to learn that her stuff does stink. Tiff had to learn, she is no better than the next person in Gods' eyesight. God loves us all but he hates the sin that we do. Tiff repented to God, she told God she was going to try to be a better person if he gave her Gavin; she told God she wanted him and she needed him. Tiff told God this man could lead her and she will listen to him, she will not run over him. The word submit is a strong, powerful word but she even told God she could and will learn how to submit only to Gavin because nothing but wisdom falls from this brother's mouth. Tiff told God it would be hard but she will try to live her life on Bible Principles. Tiff knows everything pertaining to life and godliness is in the word.

Tiff also promised God that she will go back to reading His word, she thought just like we need natural food to make it through the day, you also need spiritual food.

Tiff told God she will stop being nasty and looking down on people. At one time, nobody could tell Tiff anything; it had to be Tiff's way. Tiff knew how to manipulate people through the scriptures. She realized the things that moves a real man, is a woman with integrity, morals, ethics, not a man chaser, a woman who is honest, sober minded, a woman who will listen to her man, and not what her friends has to say because what works for one relationship does not work for all relationships. Tiff felt that if she would just stop pushing Gavin and just leave him alone, he would see her inward beauty as well as her outward beauty. Tiff was just so amazed to have met a man like Gavin in her lifetime. It was to Tiff, like a black man being President. She just did not think a man like Gavin was out there. Tiff told God and herself if she was blessed to get this man, this will be her last man and she will love and cherish him until the day she dies.

Chapter 8
Tiff Fantasize

If Tiff really got this man, she would answer to his every beck and call. She will cater to him; Tiff said she would be like Lurch, "you rang"!

Tiff looks forward to spending the rest of her life with Gavin, she is just that positive. Tiff is not desperate for a man but she is just desperate for Gavin. He is the kind of man that Tiff has always wanted, and longed for and needed.

Tiff fantasizes about a good fruitful life with Gavin, also about a life with Gavin on the highest mountain, with one house, a housekeeper: ugly, old, and fat. The only attractive person in Gavin's world will be me. They will have so much fun they will not have time to be bored. Gavin will have all silk pajamas and robes, when he gets up he will have his coffee and get on his laptop. Gavin will tell her that he is going into town. Tiff is running to get herself together so she can go with Gavin; she is grabbing her big hat and sunglasses. When Gavin gets to the car, Tiff is already in the car waiting for him.

Gavin looks at Tiff and smiles, telling her he will be gone all day. Tiff tells Gavin it is all right with her, as long as she is with him. She thinks about while they are off the mountain they will go to a nice restaurant, it might be full of people but when Gavin and Tiff are in a place, it's like nobody is there except the two of them.

Back to Reality: It was getting close to the Christmas holidays. Tiff still has not gotten anywhere with Gavin. Tiff missed Gavin so much; it just made her sick not to be with him. As Tiff lay in bed thinking about Gavin, she said to herself, Gavin is just a nice kind man to everybody. He has never been rude to me. As Tiff thought about it, she thought maybe, if she pissed Gavin off and he come back at her then he will show Tiff a side that she did not know he had. Gavin reminds Tiff of Obama, when he was running for President, they did everything in their power to make him angry but they could not.

Tiff made up her mind to stop chasing Gavin Yes, he is so precious, so sweet, so nice, so kind, so giving, so sexy, so smart, so brilliant, so together.

Tiff thought, he was not all of that, sure his smile is sweet and warm, he does have three flourishing businesses, yes he does have pretty lips, with the mustache half covering his lips. Yes, his butt is fine, wallet thick; yes, he is all of that.

Tiff buys no gifts; she just popped popcorn and watched old movies. As Tiff goes to bed on Christmas Eve, she tossed and turned all night wanting to know how will Gavin love her and when will Gavin make love to her. As Tiff lay in bed, she thinks about Gavin. Tiff wondered how it would feel to have Gavin in her arms. Gavin did not realize how much he turned Tiff on when he just looked at her. She tells herself one more lonely night, one more lonely Christmas.

Tiff tells Tiff, she has to find something to amuse Tiff. She has to find a way to Get Gavin out of her system. Tiff drags out of bed twelve o'clock noon and flops on the sofa. The doorbell rings, Tiff looks and panic, no makeup, no bath, Tiff said oh my God; oh my God. Tiff did not have time to take a bath, put on makeup, nothing, it was Gavin with Tiff a present and flowers.

THE END

"He who finds a wife finds a good thing.
And obtains favor from the Lord"
Proverbs 18:22

A Preacher's Daughter Looking for Love
Written by: J. Delores Williams

Published By:

Anderson Inc.
Publishing
P O Box 37881

Jacksonville, Fl. 32236

Special Thanks To:

Anderson Games
www.Play2Business.com

Bring your family back to the dining room table with fun games.

A family that plays together stays together.

A board game for the entire family.

Corporate Ladder Board Game is fun, educational and entertaining. This game is a stepping-stone into the world of business within the corporate structure. Corporate Ladder Game may help others change their lives from those that are easily manipulated ("followers") into those who are the go-getters ("leaders").

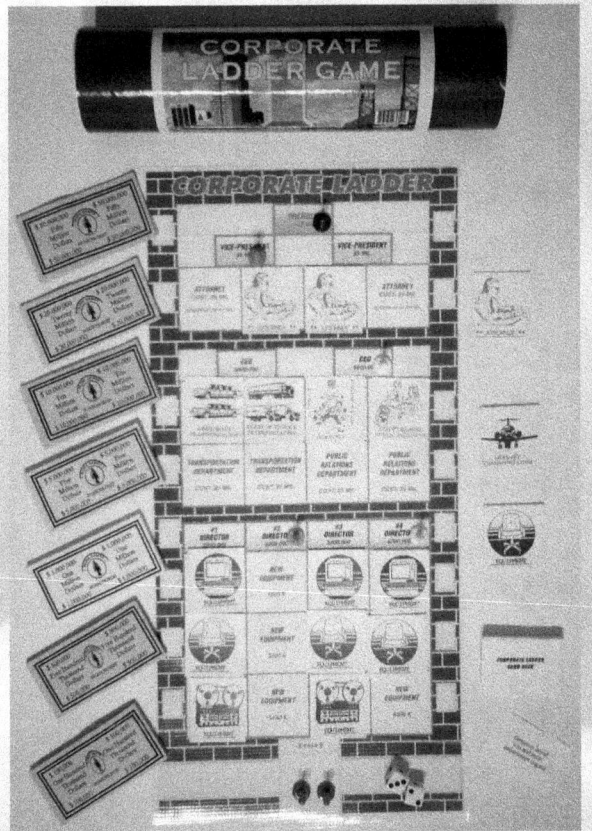

www.Play2Business.com

Go to www.Play2Business.com
or
Mail checks or money orders to:
Anderson Inc. Publishing
P.O. Box 37881
Jacksonville, FL 32236

Please send _____ copy (ies) of

A Preacher's Daughter Looking for Love

To: _____

Address: _____

City: _____ State: ____ Zip: _____

Phone:
( ) _____ / _____

Email: _____

I have enclosed $20.00 per book plus $2.00 for

S&H, a total of $ _____.

For bulk orders, wholesale rates, or appearances, you can reach us at andersoninc@netzero.com or write to:

Anderson Inc. Publishing
P.O. Box 37881
Jacksonville, FL 32236

www.ingramcontent.com/pod-product-compliance
Lightning Source LLC
Chambersburg PA
CBHW050645160426
43194CB00010B/1816